THIRD REVOLUTION IN INDIAN PERSPECTIVE

About the Author

V. S. Gupta, presently professor at the Haryana Agricultural University, had earlier worked in several media related positions in the University. Besides having worked as Editor, he headed the Farm Information and Communication Service from 1973-76 and the Public Relations Office thereafter.

He was awarded the UNDP Fellowship for training in Europe and was selected for the Journalist Fellowship Award for working in the areas of Environment and Development. Prof. Gupta has presented and published a number of papers in seminars and conferences in India and abroad. He has contributed more than fifty papers in academic journals and newspapers. In collaboration with Ranjit Singh he had edited *Communication Planning for Socio-economic Development* (1994) and with M. R. Dua *Media and Development* (1994). He represents AMIC as the Zonal Representative in North India.

He has to his credit a number of books and monographs which have been acclaimed in the national press and academic journals and have received highly favourable reviews.

THIRD REVOLUTION IN INDIAN PERSPECTIVE

Contemporary Issues and Themes in Communication

V. S. GUPTA

CONCEPT PUBLISHING COMPANY, NEW DELHI - 110 059

ISBN 81-7022-559-0

First Published 1995

Published and Printed by
Ashok Kumar Mittal
Concept Publishing Company
A/15-16, Commercial Block, Mohan Garden
NEW DELHI-110 059 (India)

Foreword

The information revolution has a crucial role to play in the transformation of economic and social paradigms and values. As is now widely acknowledged, media—being all-pervasive and extremely powerful—can catalyse and accelerate socio-economic development within developing countries. Experts in the field of development communication have made repeated attempts to disseminate information on this subject to the masses, but the field is vast and the tasks facing development communication experts are obviously daunting.

The rapid proliferation and progress of telecommunication and media technologies in recent years—and their socio-cultural impact—are subjects that have been widely discussed and debated at various levels and at numerous conferences and seminars worldwide. The electronic media's preoccupation with violence and vulgarity is a subject of serious concern, as is the widening gulf between the informed and the uninformed. Other issues that have been accorded priority are those of women's empowerment, rural development and environmental protection, and the manner in which the application of media could help to sensitise public opinion in these areas. Such themes—which are of contemporary relevance in the Indian context—have been presented in this book by Prof. V. S. Gupta.

This volume will make a valuable contribution to the current debate on media development and related issues and themes.

DR. HEINZ BONGARTZ
Resident Representative
Friedrich-Ebert-Stiftung
New Delhi

Foreword

Preface

The significance of the launching of the Early Bird satellite by the U. S. scientists in May 1965 was heralded by the Time as a 'miracle of delicate, electronics and advanced space craftsmanship'. The importance of the occasion was underscored by giving the event Cover Story status—The Communications Explosion; Early Bird and After. Visualising a startling communication explosion ahead, the analysis predicted world wide telephoning becoming common place, facsimile and data transmission, vast computer networking as also several kinds of entertainment offering choice of programmes.

The three decades after the above event have witnessed a rapid—almost mind-boggling proliferation of new information and communication technologies so much so that there have been profound and fundamental changes in almost every sphere of human activity : Life styles, entertainment, work culture, and modes of communication. The changes have been so diverse and multi-dimensional that it has not been possible to define precisely these rapid and fast paced developments. These profound changes and developments have been variously termed as : New Industrial Revolution, the Third Industrial Revolution, Information Age, Information Society, Space Age, Cabled Planet, Wired World, Post-Industrial Society or simply the Third Wave.

The phenomenal expansion of telecommunication and media technologies in the country during the recent years, and their socio-cultural impact, have been a topic for discussion and debate at various levels in numerous conferences and seminars. The problems of violence and vulgarity generated through electronic media have, of late, been a subject of serious concern; as also the disturbing issue of the widening gap between the information-rich and the information-poor. Equally important have been several emerging issues of our times : Rural Development, Women Empowerment, National Unity, Environmental Protection; and the way in which application of media could help sensitise public opinion on these and related aspects. All these themes, which have contemporary relevance in the national context, have been presented in the present publication.

The first chapter in the book traces developments leading to India on the threshold of Information Society, India's entry into space age, expansion of television and popularity of soap operas, profusion of VCR and now proliferation of cable television in urban areas have been explained. The second chapter looks into the socio-cultural impact and the concern it has generated in a large section of society regarding the impact that the present crop of TV and cable programmes are likely to have on young minds, as also the awareness campaigns launched by NGOs and voluntary bodies like Media Advocacy Groups and Centre for Media Studies. The subsequent chapters relate communication technologies and their relevance to the important and basic issues confronting the country at present.

The book also takes up issues like Regulatory and Legal aspects of Cable television, Communication Policies, Watch dog mechanisms, Social Marketing; and also significant milestones in media development in India including SEWA, Kheda Communication Project, etc. The attempt is to analyse contemporary trends in media development, including telecommunication, its impact on the society and steps needed to counter the negative impact of TV and cable programmes on young minds.

V. S. GUPTA

Acknowledgements

My close association with AMIC, over the years, as a member and also as a participant in several of its academic programmes, seminars and conferences; and its publications, helped me build insight and perspective on various media-related issues. Likewise the generous supply of media publications by the headquarters office of FES earlier, and the encouragement and support extended presently by its Resident Representative in New Delhi, Dr. Heinz Bongartz, has helped me in undertaking this writing project. I must, therefore, acknowledge my deep gratitude to the AMIC Secretary-General, Mr. Vijay Menon and Dr. Heinz Bongartz, on whose guidance and support I could depend all through.

The late Dr. J. C. Sharma, founder Director, Extension Education of our University, under whose leadership and guidance, I worked as the Head of the Farm Information and Communication Service and developed valuable understanding of the whole gamut of rural communication, and Mr. Anil Agarwal, Centre for Science and Environment, for whom I worked on an Environmental Project, deserve a special word of gratitude.

I must thank two of my colleagues, Vir Bala Aggarwal and Usha Chander, on the faculty of the Department of Journalism and Mass Communication at Himachal Pradesh University, Shimla; and Secretary, Development Communication, India, respectively, who have contributed chapters on Women Empowerment and Distance Education. Apart from working on several other projects, Ms Aggarwal is associated as an author in our forthcoming publication on National Media Policies.

I must also thank the University Librarian, Mr. Prem Singh, who apart from facilitating access to source material has helped me revise several chapters of the book and came up with several useful suggestions.

I place on record my appreciation for the efforts of my publisher, Mr. Ashok Kumar Mittal, for his valuable assistance in seeing the publication through well in time and in putting up with our deferred deadlines time and again.

It is hoped that this effort would contribute useful inputs and help advance further the ongoing debate on media issues, and application of media to the task of nation-building, stimulate interest in the fast expanding media technologies and related areas, as also the concerns that are being generated in the contemporary society.

1 November 1994 V. S. GUPTA

Contents

List of Abbreviations

ADO	Agriculture Development Officer
AIR	All India Radio
AMIC	Asian Mass Communication Research and Information Centre
APIBD	Asian Pacific Institute of Broadcasting Development
BBC	British Broadcasting Corporation
BES	Broadcasting Engineering Society
C-DOT	Centre for Development of Telematics
CNN	Cable News Network
COL	Commonwealth of Learning
DAB	Digital Audio Broadcasting
DPAP	Drought Prone Area Programme
DSC	Development Support Communication
ERNET	Education and Research in Network
FAO	Food and Agriculture Organisation
FES	Friedrich Ebert Stiftung
GDP	Gross Development Product
GNP	Gross National Product
HDI	Human Development Index
HYV	High Yielding Variety
IARI	Indian Agricultural Research Institute
ICDP	International Conference on Population and Development
IGNOU	Indira Gandhi National Open University
INSAT	Indian National Satellite
IPDC	International Programme for Development Communication
IRDP	Integrated Rural Development Programme
IRPA	Indian Rural Press Association

ISRO	Indian Space Research Organisation
KCP	Kheda Communication Project
MFALA	Marginal and Agriculture Labour Agency
NAMEDIA	Non-Aligned Media
NDC	National Development Council
NGO	Non-Governmental Organisation
NIMME	National Institute of Multi-Media Education
NICNET	National Information Centre Network
NPG	National Performance Gap
ORT	Oral Rehydration Therapy
RAX	Rural Automatic Exchange
RNI	Registrar of Newspapers of India
SAC	Space Application Centre
SEWA	Self Employed Women Association
SFDA	Small Farmers Development Agency
SITE	Satellite Instructional Television Experiment
STV	School Television
UNDP	United Nations Development Programme
UNESCO	United Nations Educational Scientific and Cultural Organization
VLW	Village Level Worker

1

The Third Revolution : An Indian Perspective

The significance of the launching of the Early Bird satellite by the U.S. scientists in May 1965 was heralded by the Time as 'a miracle of delicate electronics and advanced space craftsmanship.' The importance of the occasion was underscored by giving the event Cover Story-status – The Communications Explosion, Early Bird – And After. The story – the Communications Explosion that is literally enveloping the whole world – carried an assessment of what the fantastic advance in communications portends for the future and also the prospect of man's new capability to store a mass of information, and on signal, send it anywhere in the world.

Visualising a startling communications explosion ahead, the analysis predicted world wide telephoning becoming common place, facsimile and data transmission, vast computer networking as also several kinds of entertainment offering choice of programmes.

The three decades after the above event have witnessed a rapid – almost mind-boggling proliferation of new information and communication technologies so much so that there have been profound and fundamental changes in almost every sphere of human activity : life styles, entertainment, work culture, and modes of communication. The changes have been so diverse and multi-dimensional that it has not been possible to define precisely these rapid and fast paced developments.

Information Society

These profound changes and developments have been variously

termed as : New Industrial Revolution, the Third Industrial Revolution, Information Age, Information Society, Space Age, Post-modern Era, Cabled Planet, Wired World, Post-industrial Society, Scientific-technological Revolution, or simply The Third Wave.

All these terms are essentially an attempt to define various aspects and dimensions of the wide ranging and sweeping changes that the world has been witnessing over the past three decades.

The concept of 'Information Society' was used by the Japanese scholars as far back as 1964. However, according to Rogers the concept of Information Society began about 1955 in the U.S. In the Information Society, information constitutes the basic resource and information workers are the main segment of employees. Whereas the social scientists consider information society as a process of technical change, Porat (1978) describes this in terms of work force structure. In the Information Society, a majority of work force is engaged in the production, processing, transmission and distribution of information goods and services.

The bewildering advances and developments in computerised information systems have brought the industrialised nations to the brink of what some have begun to describe as post-industrial era of the information society. The centrality of information/knowledge has also been emphasised by Daniel Bell (1973). According to Bell in the post-industrial society, which he also calls information society, "knowledge and information are becoming the strategic resource and transforming agent of the post-industrial society". For Bell, information technology is the crucial lever of planned social control and change, the key to managing and administering complex societies. In the post-industrial society, processing of information will be more important than production of goods. The value of information will be increasingly recognised, as will the need for information specialists to act as guides to the vast information resources that will exist in the electronic form. The magnitude and diversity of the electronic resources will place trained information workers in great demand.

The ascendancy of information as commodity is becoming apparent even in developing countries, in that majority of labour force in quite a few of these consists of information workers. Informatization is becoming a global trend. Information is considered not only as commodity but also as a cultural and social resource. The contemporary socicty is at a point where information and wealth are practically one and the same thing; information is a commodity rather than a public service.

The Information Society has given rise to a large number of new occupations which are increasing at a mind dazzling rate. Alvin Toffler (1975), in Future Shock, lists some of them : systems analyst, console operator, coder, tape librarian—all associated with computer. When Fortune magazine, in the mid-sixties, surveyed 1003 young executives employed by American Corporations, it found that one out of three held a job that had not existed till he stepped into it.

Toffler considers contemporary societal changes and technological developments as high speed revolution, the Third Wave, which is creating a new civilization all around us. Classifying agricultural phasc as the First Wave, industrial phase as the Second Wave, he considers 'exploding change – with personal lives being torn apart, the existing social order crumbling, and a fantastic new way of life emerging on the horizon, as the Third Wave, with new life styles, new values and technologies, new modes of communication, new ideas and concepts emerging all around.

The changes that Toffler envisions are indeed sweeping. Taking up the analogy of the Third Wave, in a fascinating account, Toffler has classified de-massified media as the Third Wave Media.

The burgeoning flock of mini-circulation weeklies and bi-weeklies that serve the neighbourhood communities as against mass circulation dailies, leading to segmentation of the reading public, larger number of radio stations leading to specialised audience segments and citizens band radio making it possible for the listeners to communicate, Cable television which de-massifies the audience—all constitute the Third Wave Media. The Video Cassette players and recorders; and domestic satellites making it possible for individual television stations to form mini-networks—leading to smaller audiences and a larger multiplicity of programmes are the other constituents of the Third Wave Media – giving rise to new info-sphere alongside the new techno-sphere. The Third Wave media analysis of Toffler underlines the diversity and intensity of Information Society wherein entertainment, information and leisure are dominated by the products of Information Technology.

An other term used to explain the post-industrial changes is the Wired World or the Wired Society, which cssentially means a telecommunications network including multi-channel cable and satellite television, electronic mail and push button business transactions.

The innovations and developments bringing about fundamental changes in the society were the subject matter for the UNESCO publication, Impact of Science on Society in its 146 number. The editorial of this issue subsums the subject as under :

The first industrial revolution started at the end of the eighteenth century. This revolution was based on coal, involved the development of iron and steel manufacturing, the railway, inorganic chemistry and a range of consumer goods industries.

The foundations of a second industrial revolution were laid in the beginning of the twentieth century with petrol and electricity as the new sources of energy. Now towards the end of the twentieth century, a new industrial revolution has begun – the third revolution. The third revolution brings with it new forms of energy, new means of transportation and new methods of communication. Computer and communication technologies are the basis of this new revolution. It is characterised by "the increased and pervasive application of information technology in most advanced industrial societies and its penetration into the Third World". Information Technology essentially means convergence of computing and telecommunications.

India and the Third Revolution

The concept of Information Society got off to a slow start – a delayed response to the waves of sweeping changes in the outside world. However, the liberal policies of Prime Minister Rajiv Gandhi during 1984-89 ushered in telecommunication and computer revolution in the country. The information revolution got off to an encouraging beginning in 1980s as a consequence of government support for the development of electronic and telecommunication infrastructure.

During the last three years, the pace of diffusion of technologies, cable and satellite television has gathered momentum at a speed that newspaper articles have been frequently using terms as 'super-information explosion', 'multi-media revolution' and 'information super-high ways' in relation to developments in information technology in India.

Satellites

India's entry into space and boom in satellite capacity over the Indian skies will mean more satellite TV channels in major regional languages and better entertainment and news programmes. With increasing possibility of private entrepreneurs and industry entering the field, to create user-oriented information systems and products, the potential uses of space for information and communication are wide open.

Doordarshan is one of the few television organisations which uses domestic satellites for telecast of national and regional services. The successful launching of INSAT-2B has made it possible for Doordarshan to telecast additional TV programmes through domestic satellite; with five transponders on the satellite widening the network's horizon through five new channels.

With the launching of Asia Sat I in April 1990—the major broadcast satellite agency over the Indian airspace—a cable TV Revolution has set in. Asia Sat I's footprints cover most of Asia and parts of the Pacific. STAR TV launched the satellite television service through Asia Sat by the end of 1990. The number of STAR TV homes all over Asia increased rapidly. According to STAR TV Home Penetration Report 1993 by Frank Small and Associates, the number of STAR TV Homes by February 1993 in India was 3,300,500 which constituted 17 per cent of TV homes in the country. With STAR having decided to produce programmes in regional languages, its sweep on the Indian TV viewership is bound to expand.

Apart from Doordarshan programmes uplinked to the INSAT-2A satellite and the STAR to ASIA SAT, some other networks including CNN and Asia net uplinked to Arab Sat and Ekran also have contributed to the media hype that the country is currently witnessing.

The trail blazing efforts of STAR TV and intense competition to reach for the Asian skies, the satellite industry's revenues are expected to be in the range of $30 billion by the year 2000. According to Deodhar, Chairman of the Doordarshan's Airtime Committee, "space over Asia is becoming prime property. The booming economies of many Asian nations like India, China, Indonesia and Malaysia and their prosperous and demanding middle class have fueled a very high degree of interest in satellite communication services. The boon in satellite capacity over Indian skies will mean more satellite TV Channels in all major languages, more entertainment, more news".

Television

The expansion of television in India during the first two decades, after it began its programmes in September 1959, was excrutiatingly slow. However, it was the five-year period from 1982-87 that the Indian television saw phenomenal expansion, switched over from black to colour during the Asiads in 1982, created a television culture through popular programmes including *Hum Log*, *Buniyad* and *Ramayan*. This was also the period of diffusion of television in rural areas. Subsequently, the expansion programme got underway in terms of increase in transmission hours, diversification of programmes and installation of transmitters not only at all the state headquarters but elsewhere in the country.

Today, Doordarshan with its present network of 31 Programme Production Centres and 553 transmitters of varying power, reaching about 82 per cent of the country's population is one of the premier TV organisations in the world. The commissioning of five Satellite channels in 1993 was a major land mark. Doordarshan started Satellite Regional Language Services in ten regional languages for two and a half hours each.

Conscious of the competition from the cable television, which has seriously eroded the monopoly of Doordarshan, it has now come up with a number of popular entertainment, science, business and current affairs programmes so as to win back the viewers it had been suddenly losing to the other networks. Doordarshan is also opening up to criticism by encouraging independent discussion on media policies in its programmes like Newswatch and News Pulse. Apart from a large number of educational, science and development programmes, as also programmes for special segments of audience; Doordarshan operates telex service in Delhi to provide essential information on Airlines, Railways, Transport, Stock Market, Cultural Engagements and all types of latest national and international news including weather reports.

Cable Television

With the sudden and spectacular growth of satellite and cable television networks in the country since 1991, India is fast acquiring the attributes of an Information Society. The special edition of *India Today*, 1991 caught the spirit of the moment when it heralded the arrival of CNN in January and of Star TV in April, both in 1991 as "Easily the most dramatic revolution took place on the TV screen. 1991 was the year when India ended decades of isolation from the rest of the world." It added, "with five channels on offer and round – the clock broadcasting, prime time was now any time. The spread of cable TV had already given urban household a choice. Star TV decided to the Asian region made it multiple".

VCR

Alongwith the introduction of colour television in India during the Asiads in 1982, the rapid diffusion of VCR got underway. The VCR provides opportunity for in-house entertainment, time shifting, diversification of communication content, etc. Apart from the individual ownership of the VCR, renting of the VCRs and use in the intercity bus service are its two other characteristic features. The use and diffusion of VCRs through video parlours, video libraries and luxury hotels also added to its popularity as a medium of entertainment. The characteristic feature of the use of VCR in India has been that it is primarily used for film based entertainment programmes. Its potential use for purposes such as training and encouraging popular participation, transmitting development oriented messages, and other related purposes has remained strictly confined.

Telecommunication and Computer

Efficient, well developed and modern telecommunication system is *sine qua non* with modernity and economic growth, and is one of the important critical inputs to determine the progress and the pace of socio-economic transformation of the society.

Although in the previous Five Year Plans, telecommunication had made considerable strides both in quantity and quality, its growth in India as compared to the developments in the world telecommunication can at best be termed as modest. Even by the standards of many developing countries, India is far behind in providing telecom services to the people. According to Planning Commission, the telephone density in the country at 0.81 per hundred is less than that in China (1.7), Egypt (5.1), Malaysia (7.37) or even Thailand (6). Large population and the huge size of the country have adversely affected the telephone density in India inspite of the fact that telecom network has recorded considerable growth in the recent past, which was the outcome of the liberal policies of Prime Minister Rajiv Gandhi. The National Telecommunication Policy, announced in May 1994, has revised the goal to provide a telephone on demand by 1997, besides other value-added services made possible by a combination of digital switching and fibre optic transmission. It is also envisaged to provide a range of value-added services : E-mail services, audio and video conferencing services, videotext, and bureaufax centres at the sub-divisional or equivalent towns.

This fundamental shift in the priorities has been because telecommunication services are no longer considered elite services. The simplistic thinking : "A man can live without a telephone, but can he survive without drinking water", came in the way of the development of the telecommunication sector. Now the enormous planning and logistics support that an efficient telecom section can provide to all sectors of economy, and the resultant gain in productivity is being duly taken into account in determining priorities.

The experience and insight gained as a result of pilot project in Kittur village in Karnataka state in which the C-DOT provided a 128-line RAX in mid 1986, has reinforced the appreciation that telephones are something of a business necessity rather than a luxury.

A recent study of 199 villages attached to 32 C-DOT RAXs conducted by the National Council for Applied Economic Research estimates Rs. 70,000 net economic benefit from each rural telecom line. The flow of information from distant markets might permit new cropping patterns which in turn would generate higher incomes; or access to information might lead to reduction of inventories which would translate to higher profits.

A quiet revolution in computers got underway during the late nineties. The revolution, inspired by Rajiv Gandhi; the computers were all over several government offices, companies and in utility services. In a cover story, *India Today*, in its issue of 31 December 1987 highlighted the way computer had begun revolutionising the life styles in homes, in offices, in business and elsewhere. It observed : The computer is proving to be as revolutionary as the wheel. It is now put to such myriad uses as sending electronic mail, forecasting weather, scrutinising tax returns, designing buildings, in short it has whirred its way into every aspect of daily life, resulting in enormous saving of time and increasing efficiency.

NICNET is the most visible, the most ambitious computer based network of the government. The nationwide information network, NICNET, is a satellite based information service developed for its operations at the central, state and district levels. The network helps decision-making for social, economic and development planning and implementation and project monitoring. It represents an advanced level institutional application of information technology to planning and provides a model of a centrally planned approach to information services. Several other networks have also been pressed into service thus widening the base for accessing remote information and communication through electronic mail, computer conferencing, teletext, facsimile, etc.

The two important research and cooperative computer networks which India is making use are : CARINET, a network among development related organizations around the world (including Australia, Canada, Japan, Philippines, Singapore) providing information related to agriculture, health education, human rights, disaster relief, etc; and ERNET, an experimental network linking academic and research institutions in India.

Given the size of information explosion, computer in India has established its primacy as an indispensable tool for monitoring and planning development plans. The computer revolution, sweeping the country, has made its impact felt even in the hinterland districts where mass of data generated are gathered and organised for decision-making at state level.

In a paper – Information Society in their minds : A survey of college students in seven nations, Georgette Wang listed ten new media : one way and interactive cable television, video cassette recorders, video disc players, videotext, teletext, facsimile, personal computers, direct broadcast satellite and cellular radios. The paper discussed the results of a survey conducted in 1987 among 1308 college students from Hong Kong, India, Japan, Korea, Malaysia,

Singapore, Taiwan and U.S. The students in India belonged to the Delhi and Jawaharlal Nehru Universities. Although the study was explorative in nature, yet it was concluded that the Indian respondents did not feel that technologies can do much to solve the most serious national problems which in India's case were identified as, poverty, education and regional politics.

During the past decade, most of the telecom, computer and micro-electronic technologies which constitute the bed rock of Information Society, have expanded rapidly in the country. The high technology development has been aided by India's vast pool of technically trained and scientific man power, wave of liberalisation in economic policies, virtually sweeping the country and trend towards market economy. This expansion, however, is confined to largely metropolitan towns, and in some cases state headquarters and large towns in the provinces.

A very large percentage of the population, living in small towns and villages is not touched by these developments, raising several socio-cultural and economic issues, which have to be reckoned with. The extent to which beneficient aspects, which some of these technologies claim for society, could find application in nation building activities, need closer examination. Do we have adequate communication policies, monitoring and regulatory mechanisms so as to dovetail with larger national issues? Do these developments help national unity or do they widen the gap between the information rich and the information poor? Do we accept these technologies uncritically or adapt them to enhance social concerns, and protect local culture? Do we have legends, success stories and cases where communication for development or development communication could be adequately harnessed for the larger social purposes such as rural development, empowerment of women and environmental protection?

Media issues have taken centre stage for quite some time now : whether foreign media be allowed entry in the country, cultural alienation and how do we regulate onslaught from satellite and cable television on our culture and life styles which are fast becoming consumerist and commercialised. These are the questions of our times which elicit an informed discussion. Whereas it may not be possible to check the onward march of media technology, nor there is need to do so, it certainly devolves on media professionals and scholars to suggest mid-term corrections, sensitive public awareness and evolve strategies and proposals – even if that means reinforcing some earlier formulations to see that information revolution in India does not remain confined to the urban educated elites of the society and is tuned to the larger societal objectives and nation building activities.

Note

The term 'communications' has been referred to as such only where it has been used in the context of the relevant text.

REFERENCES

AMIC (1985). Satellite Technology : The Communication Equaliser, Singapore.

Bell, D. (1973) *The Coming of post industrial society: A venture in social forecasting.* New York: Basic Books.

Chatterjee, Saibal (1993). Fast forward – Special Report. *Times of India*, October 31.

Friedrich Ebert Stiftung, Bonn (1976). Mass Media in the future. Mass Media Manual

Friedrich Ebert Stiftung, Bonn (1984). New communication technologies and their impact on western industrialized countries. Communication Manual.

Goonasekera, Anura (1993). Media technology and social imperatives : An examination of communication policies in selected Asian countries. *Media Asia*, 20(4) : 194-204.

Hudson, Heather E. (1993). Maximizing benefits from new telecommunication technologies : A development based approach to communications planning. *Media Asia*, 20(3) : 133-149.

Jamias, Juan F. (1993). The impact of new communication technologies on cultural identity in rural Asia. *Media Asia* 20(4) : 205-207.

Jussawalla, Meheroo (1993). Information technology and economic development in the Asia-Pacific. *Media Asia*, 20(3) : 127-132

Khan, Rahat Nabi (1987). The third industrial revolution : An economic overview. *Impact of Science on Society*, 146 : 115-122, UNESCO.

Lee, Chang Seek and Ely D.Gomez (1992). The contribution of the information sector to the industrial growth of Korea. *Media Asia*, 19(3) : 156-168.

Mehta, Achal (1988). Harnessing new communication technologies for development in Asia. *Media Asia,* 15(2) : 63-67.

Mowlana, Hamid and Laurie, Wilson J. (1988). Communication Technology and Development. Reports and Papers on Mass Communication No. 101 : UNESCO.

Rao, P.V. (1994). High way to nowhere. *Indian Express*, July 21.

Singhal, Arvind and Rogers, Everett, M. (1989). India's Information Revolution, New Delhi: Sage.

Smith, Roger, B. (1987). The twentyfirst century corporation. *Impact of Science on Society*, 146 : 177-182, UNESCO.

Thomas, P.N. (1993). Informatization and change in India – Cultural politics in a post-modern era. *Asian Journal of Communication*, 3(1) : 64-83.

Thomas, Sunny (1994). Information highways to success. *Times of India*, June 22.

Toffler, Alvin (1975), *Future shock.* London : Pan Books.

Toffler, Alvin (1981). *The Third Wave*. London : William Collins.

UNESCO (1982). Many Voices, one world. The International Commission on the Study of Communication Problems.

Wang, Georgette (1991). Information society in their mind : A survey of college students in seven nations. *Asian Journal of Communication*, 1(2) : 1-18.

Wang, Georgette (1993). Satellite television and the future of broadcast television in the Asia-Pacific. *Media Asia*, 20(1) : 140-151.

2

Media Technologies and Socio-Cultural Imperatives

The burgeoning and bustling media industry, the rapid in-roads being made by television in the semi-urban and rural areas, fast expanding cable and satellite channels in the metropolitan and large towns; the socio-cultural implications, expression of concern by the professionals, informed and aware sections of the society – the media groups, academics and sociologists, over the media impact on life styles and habits of people, particularly the youth, have pushed media issues to the centre stage of national agenda.

These issues are no longer the close preserve of philosophical and academic discussion within the precincts of the departments and institutes of mass communication or the subject matter for deliberations in conferences and seminars. These issues including the implications of the entry of foreign media in the country have suddenly become live issues. It is, therefore, imperative to look at, however tentatively, the issues and forces unleashed by the media : gap between the information rich and the information poor, social inequity, cultural alienation, vulgarity and violence, consumerism sweeping the middle classes with the ferocity of a tidal wave.

The colour and drama of the beginnings of the 'New TV Superbazzar' was captured by the *India Today* :

> The force is with us. The mundane television set has suddenly turned into an incredible technicolour dreamboat. The remote control has placed a glitzy new world at our fingertips. Enormous metallic objects crammed with electronic gizmos circling the sky, are beaming down a bewildering collage of

> images. And like a lost tribe discovering an oasis in the desert, lakhs of Indians are hot-wired into this superbazaar of soaps, sports, news, musci sex and much more . . . Hungry for any kind of news or entertainment, lakhs of people in cities and towns across the nation are now only too familiar with the names of the new electronic media companies, an alphabet soup of initials promising round the clock nourishment – MTV, CNN, BBC, WST, CFI, TV-5, ATN, Zee TV, even PTV.

Today, an Indian viewer has access to over ten channels, as against only one a little over two years ago; and according to the present projections, by next year, he will have as many as thirty channels – as also globalisation of Doordarshan. Alongwith the technological advances in satellite and cable TV, the radio is also poised to march ahead in the hi-tech era. The DAB and radio paging will ensure that cable radio will bring Hyderabad and Houston, Madras and Moscow on the same wavelength. Dazzling indeed as these developments are, we cannot afford to just get mesmerised so as to lose the larger perspective – the socio-cultural implications of these developments.

Development has always been the catch-phrase, the *mantra*, whenever justification had to be found for introducing modern communication technologies. In the seventies, the objective of using television as an instructional and development medium appealed both to the policy planners and development experts. In India also television was introduced to harness its potential for social education, and to make it as an instrument to support the strategy and programmes of social, cultural and economic development – as a weapon against illiteracy and ignorance, for creating civic consciousness and for moulding public taste to higher aesthetic levels. The Seminar on Software Objectives of Indian Television held in New Delhi in February 1973 recommended: Television must be used in the development process as an instrument of social change and national cohesion by unhesitatingly upholding progressive values and involving the community in a free dialogue. Indian TV has to shun an elitist approach and consumer value system and evolve a true national model.

Today, however, television programming decisions are influenced by the elite middle class, who wants more entertainment and have less need for educational programmes. This urban bias of commercial television widens the gap between the rich and the poor. This dichotomy between precept and practice, rhetoric and substance, created several areas of unforeseen, but serious, socio-cultural tensions and unrest in the society.

Dichotomy and Dualism

Widening gap

According to Karnik and Chitnis (1984), our communication practice reflects the powerful pressure of the *nouveau-riche*; and that communication has played an important role in promoting a value system corresponding to the style of life of the most aggressive sections of this new class. Sexist and sadistic violence, glorification of the ruthless go-getter, lure of the latest material gadgets are almost idolised by the emerging software linked with commercial agencies.

During the eighties, in spite of badly produced programmes and a heavy and regular dose of government publicity, a whole nation became addicted to the television. Soap and religious operas like *Hum Log, Buniyaad, Ramayan* and *Mahabharat*, attracted almost cent per cent viewership. Socialising and other serious pursuits such as reading became casualities as television, and to a lesser extent, video monopolised all available leisure time.

In his paper: National Cost of Television in India in the Year 2000 : Socio-Economic and Political Implications and Issues, Srivastava (1987) has concluded :

1. As urban viewers would constitute the majority of the viewers, they would demand the kinds of programmes which are entertainment based, rather than those which play the role of a development communication tool.

2. There will be perpetual conflict between programmes meant for rural and urban poor and those suitable for middle and upper income brackets in urban areas.

3. In terms of political implications, the vast majority of rural masses would not have access to TV. Thus, the TV's role for integration and unity of the country and as an equaliser of regional differences would not be achieved.

4. The people who would have access to TV would already have high media exposure from newspapers, radio, video and movies. The

media poor would not be able to afford most of the means of receiving external information through electronic media. Thus, the knowledge gap between haves and have nots would widen.

The eminent sociologist, Kothari (1993), in Growing Amnesia, has highlighted the fact that the state is playing an increasingly diminishing interventionist role and it has been left to be decided by the market forces as to what is good for the people. Pointing out to the burgeoning consumerist society which is only concerned with the gratification of individuals, Kothari says : social equity has been, for all practical purposes, sacrificed at the altar of development models that are designed to modernise society in terms of technology and science*.

In this context Kishore (1994) points out : The middle class elite in India whose life styles resemble that of the super-rich anywhere in the world are at a comparative advantage over access to information and entertainment. The internal contradictions in present day India are stark clear : industrialized cities and marginally subsistent villages; jet planes and bullock carts; satellite technology and lack of clean drinking water, cellular telephones and the absence of even one telephone in every village. This dualism has widened the gap between the rich and the poor.

Since early 1960s, India has been keen on using satellite communication for national development. The late Dr. Vikram Sarabhai, who had initiated the SITE Project was of the opinion that developing nations such as India have the possibility of using effectively space communication for national needs. Satellite television bridges physical distances to reach the rural and the remote.

However, articulating his apprehensions of extending and perpetuating the hegemony by dominating powers, Jayaweera (1982) in a scintillating discussion on : Communication Satellites – A Third World Perspective, puts forward forcefully and forthrightly his case that satellite technology after all may not have the potential that it is credited with, on the other hand it might consolidate and perpetuate the inequities rather than redressing.

In the above discussion, Jayaweera leads forth the debate whether satellites can meet the principal needs they are credited with. The brief summary given in the tabular form focuses

---

**Pioneer*, 11 December, 1993

Jayaweera's views adequately.

Oversell of Media Technology

It is, therefore, essential to emphasize the need of not accepting facile and uncritical assumptions underlying proliferation of media technology without having a close look at their socio-economic implications. Also to underline the fact that technology is no easy substitute for the long, hard way that lies ahead for a development planner to transverse.

Relevance of communication satellites to development : claims	Reconsideration of these claims
1. *National integration* Many Third World countries, either by reason of their immensity and geographical dispersal like India and Indonesia, or by reason of their heterogeneous social composition or because of natural barriers like vast expenses of forests, deserts or mountains are yet to be integrated into a single polity. Domestic distribution satellites can perform this function much more cost effectively.	1. *National integration* Lack of national integration is far more complex than is suggested by territorial vastness or the incidence of forests, mountains and deserts. Very often there is need for more autonomy for the constituent national entities. In such situations satellites can be used either as instruments of coercion or as a substitute for more human forms of achieving integration.
2. *Administrative effectiveness* As a corollary to 1 above, administrative integration and effectiveness is hampered. The bureaucracy tends towards concentration and higher effectiveness in the metropolis, and declines outwards.	2. *Administrative effectiveness* Bureaucratic concentration in the metropolis, which is largely responsible for administrative ineffectiveness in the Third World, is likely to be aggravated through a communication satellite.
3. *Delivery of education, both formal and non-formal including teacher training* The shortage of schools, teachers, equipment and buildings is chronic in most Third World countries. Satellites have the capacity to multiply these meagre resources at a fraction of their terrestrial costs.	3. *Delivery of education* This slogan has been used consistently to justify the introduction of TV into the Third World. TV is recommended to the Third World not for entertainment, or for commerce, but for education. For over two decades experiments have been conducted for determining

	the adequacy of TV as a vehicle for education. However, there is considerable evidence to show that education is best delivered in a face-to-face inter-active situation.
4. *Delivery of agricultural extension* As in the area of education, effective agricultural extension work is hampered by the lack of trained extension workers, the lack of transport, the inability to have as many demonstration plots as are needed, etc. All this can be overcome through satellites.	4. *Delivery of agricultural extension* The problem of agricultural extension in Third World countries is more than a question of access to knowledge, and demonstration. It is primarily a question of land tenure, the lack of credit, the lack of irrigation facilities, the high cost of inputs, etc. Most of these are structural and political questions.
5. *Delivery of family planning programmes* It is claimed by many development economists that the greatest single impediment to development in the Third World is population growth which every year either outstrips or at least equals economic growth. Family planning is therefore seen by them to constitute the center-piece of any long term economic strategy. But the crucial question underlying all family planning programmes is the one concerning communication. It is claimed that satellites are the answer.	5. *Delivery of family planning programmes* The considerations that apply to education apply here too.
6. *Delivery of medical and health care services* What has been said of educational, agricultural and family planning extension is equally true of medical and health care. The same infra-structural and personnel inadequacies baulk the delivery of adequate diagnostic and curative services from the metropolis, where a certain volume of professional skills is concentrated, to the outlying provinces where they are grossly inadequate or totally absent.	6. *Delivery of medical and health care* The fundamental issues of medical and health care in the Third World are not related to the lack of communication but have to do with the lack of clean drinking water and the lack of protein and vitamins. They are not diagnostic but directly stemming from poverty.

7. *Isolation from marketing information, both national and international* A modern economy must have access to and supply data, the most up-to-date, instantaneously and on call both to suppliers and customers, abroad and at home. Unless entrepreneurs, banks and firms have access to data banks and facsimile services through computers linked to satellites using digital transmissions, the international market would collapse. On a much smaller scale, this would be equally true of the domestic market.	7. *Isolation from marketing information* This is a disability peculiar to big entrepreneurs and multinational corporations based in Third World metropolitan centres and not a felt need among small-holding subsistence farmers and village cooperatives who constitute the bulk of the rural sector. The solution to the latter's need for fair prices is not likely to be provided by instantaneous satellite communication.
8. *Participation as a development tool* Most Third World societies are highly hierarchical. Planning and decision making are centralised and removed from the people. There are neither political nor societal mechanisms that enable the widest possible community to participate in either the political or the production process. This is one of the reasons attributed to account for low productivity in these societies. Normally, securing participation in broad societal processes is a highly complicated enterprise in social engineering. But technologists see in communication satellites the final answer.	8. *Participation* Like pluralism, participation is a product of political consciousness, of the pressure of organised and motivated people on the structures of power. It can never be contrived, least by recourse to technological devices.

The above table is reproduced from the paper, Media Technologies and Socio-Economic Imperatives—An Indian Perspective—Vir Bala and V.S. Gupta, published in *Communication Planning for Socio-Economic Development* (1994).

Video — the Wonder Child of Communication

After television and satellites let us take a close look at another wonder child of modern communication technology — Video.

In the initial stages of video proliferation, it was hoped that video would provide development messages tailored to individuals and groups in a way that is not possible with television and radio, encourage popular participation, knowledge-sharing, and facilitate self-development efforts by individuals, groups and communities. In addition to providing entertainment, VCRs can also serve an important role in education and training. However, it is now a well established fact that video in India is used in a very limited way for education and development purposes; such as teacher's training programmes and in the training of business and public leaders. While VCR technology has high potential for use in development, this potential has remained unrealized.

Leela Rao (1987) says : Much like its predecessor, the television, video just happened in India. The 'revolution' was confined to the flooding of hardware into a ready and expectant consumer market. There was no supporting software ideology or an independent cultural identity of the new medium. In such a situation, video is part of a vastly 'popular culture' – the Indian feature film was inevitable and immediate. It, therefore, appears presumptuous to talk of a video revolution, whereas for all practical purposes influence of the new medium has primarily been to modify and redefine the marketing methods of an older product – the commercial feature film. Video has not in any way diversified the content of communication, nor brought in newer frontiers of knowledge and experience within the reach of its consumers. If anything, it has further enhanced and consolidated the Indian feature film as the most consistent primary source of mass culture.

It also seems to strengthen the concern that emerging technologies would widen the gaps rather than provide a bridge; and that the newer categories of haves and have-nots may centre around the criteria of access to video. But in terms of defining the utilisation of the video technology, the viewers appear to have an undivided understanding – that its primary function is entertainment.

The conclusion is unmistakable : Video technology provides mostly entertainment and its potential for development lies generally untapped.

Cable Television

Much like the above communication technologies – development of cable television was also heralded as 'an answer to the need for more diversified content', since cable television offers the possibility of unlimited number of channels for a multiplicity of users and purposes (multiple channels, multiple choices for the viewer) it was trumpted as "technology of abundance". It was, however, not adequately realised that cable television could not be optimally used unless there are a number of stations with a variety of programme material available to feed those channels. In the absence of sufficient quantity of culturally compatible, civic and community oriented software available, the cable operators have to fall back upon whatever is available in the entertainment supermarket.

We would be deluding ourselves if we think that the problem of cultural alienation through cable television is basically limited to the elite class; because it is the elites who guide and govern the important decisions in the government and it is important to consider how their value system is developed.

In the Report of the International Commission for the Study of Communication Problems, it has been stated that introduction of cable television has profound effects on the existing broadcasting situation. Capital investment in cable hardware may constitute "more of a privilege of the affluent urban dweller than a realistic option for more than three quarters of the world's population." Some countries that have introduced cable television note its detrimental effect on "cultural sovereignty."

In this context, some of the relevant observations in the Report are reproduced :

> The promise of cable television (multiple channels, multiple choices for the viewer) may have been oversold in the early development period. There were high expectations that community access channels would enrich community life by fostering communication among individuals and community groups, provide new forum for neighbourhood dialogue and artistic expression; revolutionize the communication patterns of service organizations, consumer groups and political parties. In fact, cable television's provision of the community access channel was hailed as the technology that would personalize the electronic media and create a sense of community in urban settings, which had been depersonalized by the advances of other technologies.

Glorification of media technology could not have gone any further. As referred to above, cable was once trumpted as the "technology of abundance," a medium so expansive that no social engineering would be needed for a multitude of tongues to flourish. As Pradip N. Thomas, in his paper, Informatization and Change in India – Cultural Politics in a Post-Modern Era (1993) states : But this turned out to be an other instance in a long standing tradition of blind optimism in technologies to bring about social change.

The Thrill Syndrome and Cultural Invasion

Although cable television has been with us only for a little over three years, mostly in metropolitan cities, search is already on for finding out "antidote" in order to counter its deleterious effects.

Any concerned citizen will feel greatly alarmed when a leading national newspaper* in its first lead story, highlighted the search that the schools and parents desperately mounted looking for an antidote to satellite television. Disturbed that the students in Delhi's elite schools were not keeping up with their studies and general knowledge, a teacher decided to take a close look at the reading habits of her students. She found that they have been spending upto four hours each day watching programmes which provided them entertainment, rather than education or general knowledge; television provided them with thrill. The thrill syndrome has resulted in behavioural abnormalities, reading and writing much less and generally suffering from under exposure to print. The Forum of Public Schools representing 60-odd institutions, which met to discuss how violence and promiscuity on the screen are affecting student behaviour, found out that the above trend is already causing passivity among children, leading to physical and mental retardation. As a consequence, several parents decided to get the cable disconnected.

Reacting strongly against the role of media in promoting vulgarity and stifling the mental growth of children without due regard to moral propriety, the teachers belonging to the Forum for Public Schools in New Delhi have given a call for "Quit India" and said no to the cultural invasion. The over-indulgent multinational culture promoted by these programmes is leading to an increase in

---

* *Times of India*, 15 November, 1993

incidence of crime among the adolescents and a virtual compromise of cultural identity, said a group of teachers at a joint press conference. The teachers said they had resolved to oppose vulgarity and violence tooth and nail so that tendencies towards lasciviousness which films and advertisements tend to incite could be curbed. The teachers said mindless consumerism being promoted in the country at the behest of the multinationals who want to protect their interests was responsible for the cultural invasion in the form of these ads*.

An independent survey conducted by the *Times of India* in the metropolitan cities revealed that cinema and soap operas have currently become an addiction with the teenagers with an upper middle class background. Their favourite heroes turn out to be one famous for their propensity for militant action as the answer to all evils. The action today obviously is on aggression, says the survey.

The Special Report on Teen Spirit, referring to a landmark study of 400 American teenagers by Dr. L. Rowell Huesman and Leonard Eron of University of Illinois concludes that "heavy exposure to televised violence is one of the causes of aggressive behaviour, crime and violence in society. TV violence affects youngsters of all ages of both genders, at all socio-economic levels and all levels of intelligence."

Rising concern about juvenile delinquency, crime and general unrest and its relationship with television led to investigations by several committees and Media Task Force set up by the US Administration.

The Cultural Indicators Research Project developed a concept of television violence which concluded : For most groups of viewers, television's mean and dangerous world tends to cultivate a relative sense of fear, victimization, mistrust, insecurity, and dependence, and despite its supposedly 'entertaining' nature – of alienation and gloom.

The lines of research that provide some answer to the broader question of media violence and the impact it might create to different patterns of thinking and action, emerged from large scale projects of 1970 and 1980. They suggest that the violence terror scenario may have several consequences which include the cultivation of aggressive tendencies, the accommodation to violence, the depersonalization and isolation of offenders, the sporadic triggering

---

**Hindu,* 31 July, 1994

of violent acts, and the levels of vulnerability and dependence felt by different groups living with the images of a mean and dangerous world.

Writing about the contemporary Indian society it has been observed : A society of growing violence will probably be an adequate summing up of the contemporary Indian society. Growing caste and communal violence, violence in the family as reflected in the increasing number of dowry deaths and at the cultural sphere, violence shown in popular mass media, indicate how crucial areas of social life are endangered by brutality and turbulence. Of a different kind, but equally significant is the violence engineered by the state. In short, violence has come to characterise a society which is mythically assumed to be both pietist and pacific.*

That television has debased popular taste and offers fare that caters to the least common denominator and homogenized popular culture is widely accepted. Referring to the mini review of a book, Carnival Culture : the trashing of taste in America by James B. Twitchell, Sayani (1993) says : According to Twitchell, the three great purveyors of mass culture in the United States – book publishing, motion pictures and television – are creating a culture that glorifies the vulgar and mediocre at the expense of worthwhile qualities in American life. He argues that the media has raised the "low-brow" to a level of respectability that excludes what used to be high-brow from American life.

It is indeed amusing, if not worrying, to find out that whereas in USA there is concern about debasement of the American culture, the Third World countries are facing the onslaught of the alien culture. Sen (1993) points out : Media and cultural products carry innate values of the place of origination. One of the cultural issues is the possible promotion of consumerism and cultural homogeneity by imitating or outright acceptance of the commercial American model of production and programming thus spreading alien cultural values.

Alarmed by the vulgarity and crass low taste displayed by songs like *Choli Kay Peechhay Kai Hai*, which had outraged public opinion and agitated the minds of the members of Parliament, the Ministry of Information and Broadcasting, film industry, film critics and

---

* Continuity and Change : Society November-December 1988, A Sesquicentunial Times of India Publication.

members of the Censor Board, decided to evolve a mechanism so as to curb the further dissemination of such songs through AIR and Doordarshan.

It needs to be noted that two years ago, concerned women media professionals set up a forum, Media Advocacy Group, to monitor mainly the electronic and broadcast media, to carry out 'impact studies', hold workshops and generally work towards making the media more inclusive, and specifically, more gender sensitive. Recently, it produced a short report on viewer feed back (the sample consisted of 371 low and middle class households in Delhi) on different television programmes. According to the report, songs like *Sexy, Sexy, Cholee Ke Peechey* were found to be obscene and objectionable. The report found that viewers were angry and disgusted at the rising level of obscenity in films*.

It is indeed a happy augury and a positive development that a group of media professionals could come together, create a forum like Media Advocacy Group and attempt sensitising public opinion on issues of import.

National Communication System

In this context it would be pertinent to take note of the observations of the International Commission for the Study of Communication Problem : Because communication is a part of culture as much as an influence upon it, the development of a national communication system can hope to foster a thriving national culture. Mass media must be fully integrated in the whole communication system, which itself display the characteristics inherent in the nation and correlate traditional and modern communication means.

It has become almost axiomatic to stress that technology is not neutral. It is good or bad, depending upon the use to which it is put. It is important that public opinion be sensitised to various aspects of the working of media and the naunces of the socio-cultural imperatives to enable it to exercise an informed and critical choice. Technology alone cannot be considered a panacea for all the problems of the country. The challenge before the media scholars, concerned groups, organisations and formations lies in enabling the

---

* *The Hindu*, 3 July, 1994, Airing Differences.

government and the people to help in absorbing, challenising and improvising technology to serve its well defined social and cultural objectives.

REFERENCES

Gerbner, George (1988). Violence and Terror in the Mass Media. Reports and Papers on Mass Communication, UNESCO.

Guback, Thomas and Varis, Topio (1982). Transnational Communication and Cultural Industries. UNESCO.

Hudson, Heather (1989). Information Technology : Challenges for Development. *Development Communication Report*, 4 (67) : 1-2.

Jayaweera, Neville D. (1982). Communication Satellites – A Third World Perspective. New Communication Technologies and their Impact on Western Industrialized Countries. Summary Report of a Colloquium held in Bonn, 17-19 December.

Karnik, K. S. and E. V. Chitnis (1984). As quoted, in : Joshi, P.C. (ed.) *Communication and Nation Building — Perspective and Policy* (1986), New Delhi : Publications Division.

Kishore, Krishna (1994). The Advent of STAR TV in India : Emerging Policy Issues *Media Asia*, 20(2) : 96-103.

Khushu, O.P. (1993). Impact of satellite communications in the Asia-Pacific region *Asian Mass Communication Bulletin*, 23(1) : 10-11.

Mehra, Achal (1988). Harnessing new communication technologies for development in Asia. *Media Asia*, 15(2) : 63-67.

Michael Kunczik (1991). Communication and Social Change. Friedrich-Ebert-Stiftung, Bonn.

Mody, Bella (1984). Technology Option for Third World countries : Do we have the freedom to choose. *Media Asia*, 11(2) : 85-89.

Rahman, M. (1992). The New TV Superbazaar – Now at Your Fingertips. *India Today*, September 15.

Rao, Leela (1987). VCR and its Influence on Life Styles in South India. *Media Asia*, 14(1) : 15-22.

Sayani, Ameen (1993). National and Transnational Censorship – Guidelines and Advertising Codes for Radio and Television. Paper presented at AMIC seminar on the Legal and Regulatory Aspects of Satellite Broadcasting, New Delhi, 22-23, October.

Sayer, John (1987). Information technology contributes to social change in Asia. *Media Development*, XXXIV(4) : 7-9.

Sen, Abhijit (1993). The Impact of American Pop Culture in the Third World. *Media Asia*, 20(4) : 208-217.

Singhal, Arvind and Rogers, Everett M. (1989). India's Information Revolution. Sage : New Delhi.

Srivastava, U.K. (1987). National cost of television in India in the year 2000 : Socio-economic and political implications and issues. *Media Asia*, 14(3) : 136-148.

Thomas, Pradip N. (1993). Informatization and Change in India – Cultural Politics in a Post-Modern Era. *Asian Journal of Communication*, 3(1) : 64-83.

Times of India (1993). Schools, parents search for antidote to satellite television.

November 15.

UNESCO (1982). Many Voices, One World. The International Commission on the Study of Communication Problems. pp. 89-90.

Vir Bala and V. S. Gupta (1994). Media Technologies and Socio Economic Imperatives - An Indian Perspective, in Gupta, V .S. and Ranjit Singh (eds.) : *Communication Planning for Socio-Economic Development*. New Delhi : Har Anand Publications, pp. 34-48.

Wang, Georgette (1991). Information Society in their Mind : A Survey of College Students in Seven Nations. *Asian Journal of Communication*, 1(2) : 1-18.

3

Communication Policies : An Overview

Communication policies are sets of legislative measures, principles, norms and directions established to guide the functioning of communication systems. The policies are shaped over time in the context of country's general approach to communication systems, emanating as they do from political ideologies; and are related to the socio-economic development of the society.

Communication policies, being fairly new concepts, are just evolving. It is primarily because the media in India, and particularly the broadcast media have grown haphazardly, and not as a part of well defined national communication policy. However, communication policies, either explicitly in constitution, legislations, codes of conduct, rules and procedures; or implicitly in accepted practices and conventions do exist at the national, institutional and professional levels.

An expert body at a meeting convened by UNESCO in Manila in 1977 considered the question of Communication Policy which may be considered to be a synonym of National Media Policy. The panel observed : A National Communication Policy means an integrated and reasonably durable set of principles, rules and guidelines to assist communication systems of a country to operate efficiently to help attain national goals. It provides a frame of reference for the elaboration of national strategies and plans for communication; infrastructures and activities, making the best use of available resources.

The Chairman of Press Council of India, Justice A. N. Sen, has however been of the opinion that it may not be wise to seek to lay down any firm National Media Policy, as the effective implementation of the policy may create more problems than it is likely to solve; although there may not be any difficulty in arriving at a general consensus as to certain norms to be observed by the media instead of seeking to lay down any firm National Media Policy.

While defining National Media Policy, Pran Chopra stated : By National Policy I am only going to mean those decisions of the national government which might help the media fulfil functions that are appropriate for them in a democratic and pluralistic country like India. I consider four functions of the media to be the most appropriate in the Indian context. First, the media should provide to the largest number of people easy access to information which is reliable, relevant, and abundant. Second, the media must provide reasonably free channels of expression for opinions which are well informed, responsible and adequately reflect all relevant points of view. Third, the media should be a two-way channel; not only addressing messages to the audience but also giving the audience a forum for the expression of its concerns. The fourth overrides all these three functions : the media must preserve their credibility. The foremost objective of a National Media Policy should be that it must open government's door a little wider for the public to get better access to reliable information.

Communication policies may be very general, in the nature of desirable goals and principles, or they may be more specific and practically binding. They may exist or be formulated at many levels. They may be incorporated in the constitution or legislation of a country, in overall national policies, in the guidelines for individual administrations, professional codes of ethics, as well as in the constitution and operation of particular communication systems, both governmental and non-governmental. They may have world-wide, regional, national or sub-national dimensions.

All national governments have at one time or the other dealt with communication policies. Some have established permanent or ad hoc organs to advise on or deal with minor or major components of such policies. If these are, by chance, not part of the declared government objectives, they may yet implicitly exist in the established relationships between government and institutions, be they broadcasting companies, newspapers, publishing houses, professional bodies, etc.

India does not have a comprehensive media policy which can

take care of all aspects of the functioning of media. The Indian media policies have, however, been influenced by two guiding principles : Article 19 of the Indian Constitution which guarantees the right to freedom of speech and expression which naturally encompasses free flow of information and therefore covers broadcasting; and the Universal Declaration of Human Rights of 1948 which says : Every one has the right to freedom of opinion and expression; this right includes freedom to hold opinions without interference and to seek, receive and impart information and ideas through any media and regardless of frontiers.

Communication Policies in the Indian context are enshrined through such regulatory and legislative mechanisms as the Broadcasting Code governing All India Radio, the Code for Commercial Advertising on Doordarshan, circulars and notifications on guidelines for news policy placed in the Indian Parliament, Reports of the Ministry of Information and Broadcasting, and laws such as Press Council Act, etc. These guidelines, alongwith the Prasar Bharati (Broadcasting Corporation of India) Act, 1990; and the Cable Television Networks (Regulation) Bill, 1993 constitute the core of communication policies in the country.

The Cable Television Networks (Regulation) Bill, 1993 is, in fact, a major initiative in the direction of providing legal aspects to cable broadcasting. On August 8 last year, the Government introduced this Bill in the Rajya Sabha. The Bill aims at regulating the operation of cable television networks in the entire country so as to bring uniformity in their operation. The vast potential of new technology is intended to be utilised for the dissemination of information and entertainment. It has been clearly recognized in the Bill that there has been a haphazard mushrooming of cable television networks all over the country during the last few years as a result of the availability of signals of foreign television networks via satellites. This has been perceived as a cultural invasion in many quarters since the programmes available on these satellite channels are predominantly western and totally alien to our culture and way of life. Since there is no regulation for these cable television networks, a lot of undesirable programmes and advertisements are becoming available to the viewers without any kind of censorship.

Likewise the Prasar Bharati Bill provides a comprehensive definition of broadcasting which says :

> Broadcasting means the dissemination of any form of communication like signs, signals, writing, pictures, images and sounds of all kinds by transmission of electromagnetic waves through space or through cables intended to be received by the general public either directly or indirectly through the medium of relay stations and all its grammatical variations and cognate expressions shall be construed accordingly.

It is more comprehensive because it takes care of the transmission of electromagnetic waves through space or through cables. The Prasar Bharati Act also aimed at creating a Broadcasting Corporation and the parameters within which this corporation was supposed to function, in fact, provide a pointer which should govern our broadcasting policies. Under Section 12(2) it was stated that the Broadcasting Corporation, envisaged under the Act, would be functioning and be guided by such objectives as : upholding the unity and integrity of the country and the values enshrined in the Constitution, safeguarding the citizen's rights to be informed freely, paying special attention to the fields of education, literacy, agriculture, environment, etc.; providing adequate coverage to the diverse cultures, informing and stimulating the national consciousness in regard to the status and problems of women, promoting social justice, safeguarding the rights of the working classes, serving the rural and weaker sections, providing suitable programmes keeping in view the special needs of the minorities and tribal communities, taking special steps to protect the interests of children, the blind, the aged and the handicapped, and other vulnerable sections of the people, promoting national integration, providing comprehensive broadcast coverage through the choice of appropriate technology, promoting research and development activities in order to ensure that radio and television broadcasting technology are constantly updated, expanding broadcasting facilities by establishing additional channels of transmission at various levels, etc.

The discussion on communication policies has been greatly enriched by the deliberations, reports and recommendations of several committees constituted by the Government of India from time to time. The mandate given to several of these committees was to examine and evaluate policies and programmes of media organisations; recommend autonomy for Akashvani and

Doordarshan and software plan for Doordarshan. The evaluation reports of the SITE, Reports and Papers on Mass Commission by UNESCO and the Report of the International Commission for the Study of Communication Problems constituted by UNESCO in 1977 have also contributed a large body of information covering the widest possible spectrum on all issues impinging upon communication and development. Salient features of reports and recommendations of some of the committees are summarised in the discussion below.

1. Committee on Broadcasting and Information Media (1964)

This committee, also popularly known as the Chanda Committee, constituted in December 1964, presented the Report on Radio and Television in April 1966. The Committee observed: It is not possible in the Indian context for a creative medium like broadcasting to flourish under a regiment (sic) of departmental rules and regulations. It is only by an institutional change that AIR can be liberated from the present rigid financial and administrative procedures of the Government. It recommended that the separate Corporations, set up for Akashvani and Doordarshan, should have the freedom to evolve its own methods of recruitment, regulate scales of pay and conditions of service according to its needs, and devise a financial and accounting system appropriate to its creative activity.

This recommendation was considered by the Cabinet in December 1969, and the Lok Sabha was informed in April 1970 that the present was not an opportune time to consider the conversion of All India Radio into an autonomous Corporation. However, another important recommendation that Akashvani and Doordarshan be separated, was accepted and took effect from April 1, 1976.

Arguing for the grant of autonomy to the two media, the Chanda Committee had said : Theoretically it (AIR) has the freedom of a national newspaper to present objectively topics of current interest but in practice it has failed to do so mainly for two reasons. First, successive ministers usurped the policy making functions of the Director General and started interfering even in matters of programme planning and presentation, and second, the selection of the directing staff was so made as to ensure unquestioning compliance. As a result the public image of AIR has become tarnished, its objectivity destroyed and its initiative gradually whittled away.

2. Satellite Instructional Television Experiment (1975)

The SITE was a one year pilot project in 1975-76, primarily undertaken to experiment with television through satellite communication to broadcast special programmes in six states which included 2400 villages. The experiment aroused wide international interest. India was the developing country in the region to undertake an experiment using space age technology to bring its millions into the mainstream of national life, make them aware of the changing pattern of present day urban life and help them to harness their resources for optimum benefits. Explaining the importance of SITE, Narayana Menon (1976), in his book, *The Communication Revolution* wrote :

> SITE means a lot of things apart from being an experiment. For one thing, it made India TV-conscious and of an advanced style of TV technology. TV is no more confined to the main metropolitan centres. It has suddenly made its presence felt in the villages of Karnataka, Andhra, Orissa, Madhya Pradesh, Bihar and Rajasthan. Hundreds of engineers, technicians and mechanics are acquiring new skills and vast experience. Programmers, broadcasters and telecasters are getting new insights into the medium. In spite of all the doubts and hesitations, bureaucratic stumbling blocks, genteel in-fighting, shortage of equipment, facilities, money, we are in the middle of a vast learning process, the culmination of the tentative approaches of the tele-club days of 1959. All these things add up to substantial investments which should, in the long run, bring rich dividends. As Vikram Sarabhai said, television is an investment rather than an overhead.

However, the former Director General of Akashvani, P. C. Chatterjee, while commenting on the achievements of SITE observed : In the practical aspects of nation building on which programmes were telecast during SITE, i.e. agriculture, animal husbandry, health and nutrition, family planning and in telecasts for schools, we find that the gains were rather meagre.

3. Working Group on Autonomy for Akashvani and Doordarshan (1977)

The committee also popularly known as Verghese Committee, appointed in August 1977 submitted its Report to the Government in February 1978. The Report is a landmark document on the aspect of granting autonomy to the electronic media. Its major recommendations were:

(i) An autonomous national trust should be established under which Akashvani and Doordarshan would function. It gave a name to the proposed authority – Akash Bharati : the National Broadcast Trust;

(ii) Radio and TV should work for the public purpose. They should function within the framework of a broad perspective of national communication policy;

(iii) The proposed autonomous broadcasting trust authority should be owned by the nation and be accountable to the Parliament;

(iv) The priority of broadcasting has to change from "urban-elitist moorings to the rural and semi-urban areas and to the urban poor". The quality of programmes would have to improve. It should also work towards filling the rural-urban and tradition modernity gaps;

(v) The idea of one autonomous corporation each for All India Radio and Doordarshan did not find support from the Working Group. It opted for one autonomous national trust for both of the broadcast media – radio and television. It also rejected the concept of autonomous regional corporations, but it envisaged decentralization of national broadcasting authority; and

(vi) The autonomy of the authority and independence from control of the government should be guaranteed by the Constitution.

The Government introduced a Bill in May 1979 which envisaged setting up of an autonomous corporation known as Prasar Bharati. Since the Government went out of office, the Bill lapsed and the successor government headed by Mrs. Indira Gandhi decided not to set up an autonomous body.

The government later on introduced the Prasar Bharati (Broadcasting Corporation of India), Act 1990 in September 1990. However, the continued foot dragging on the implementation of the Prasar Bharati Act and the yawning gap between the government's rhetoric and its practice, clearly shows that autonomy for the electronic media is as distant a dream as ever.

4. International Commission for the Study of Communication Problems (1977)

The Commission, also popularly known as MacBride Commission, was established by UNESCO to study among other issues such as increasing importance attached to communication as a social phenomenon and the consequent interest shown in the development of communication media; the growing impact and repercussions of technological progress in the field, etc. The President of the Commission, Sean MacBride, transmitted the Final Report to the Director General, UNESCO in February 1980. Some of the important recommendations of the Commission are :

(i) Communication be no longer regarded merely as an incidental service and its development left to chance. Recognition of its potential warrants the formulation by all nations, and particularly developing countries, of comprehensive communication policies linked to overall social, cultural, economic and political goals. Such policies should be based on inter-ministerial and inter-disciplinary consultations with broad public participation;

(ii) Within the frame work of national development policies, each country will have to work out its own set of priorities, bearing in mind that it will not be possible to move in all directions at the same time. But, as far as resources allow, communication policies should aim at stimulating and encouraging all means of communication;

(iii) The communication component in all development projects should receive adequate financing. So-called "development support communications" are essential for mobilizing initiatives and providing information required for action in all fields of development – agriculture, health and family planning, education, religion, industry and so on. Essential communication needs to be met include the extension of basic postal services and telecommunication networks through small rural electronic exchanges; and

(iv) Development strategies should incorporate communication policies as an integral part in the diagnosis of needs and in the design and implementation of selected priorities. In this respect communication should be considered a major development resource, a vehicle to ensure real political participation in decision making, a central information base for defining policy options, and an instrument for creating awareness of national priorities.

5. Working Group on Software Planning for Doordarshan (1983)

The Working Group, also popularly known as the Joshi Committee, was established to make recommendations regarding programming in Indian television. It submitted its report in April 1984, sub-titled as 'An Indian Personality for Television'. The report was formally laid on the table of Lok Sabha in 1985. Even though the Working Group was formed to make recommendations regarding Doordarshan, its report underlines the overall communication approach and policy concerning other sectors of mass media.

The Working Group Report made several recommendations on creating appropriate environment for the development of creative software for Doordarshan. In the first place, the Working Group was convinced that such an environment did not exist within the present structure of the organization. It was also convinced that whatever the claims of the Government, Doordarshan did not enjoy 'functional freedom' and 'the lack of such freedom is having a detrimental effect on the planning and quality of its programmes. It recommended the setting up of a National Doordarshan Council which would have three roles to perform : to review and guide the organisation's performance, as a guardian of Doordarshan's functional and professional autonomy, and as a counterpart of the Press Council for examining complaints of inaccuracy or bias in the reporting of news and comment on current affairs. The Report emphasized that a developing country like India is exposed to the danger of erosion of its national cultural identity, and the need is to resist the cultural invasion from outside through restriction of imported programmes and 'positive software planning'. It discerned a credibility gap created by the growing hiatus between profession and practice, between official policy pronouncements emphasising use of television for development and education, and the increasing drift and departure from them in actual programming. It, therefore, urged the exploitation of the 'development potential' of television, of using communication technology for 'leapfrogging into growth and development'. It endorsed the Nehru and Sarabhai approach of tapping the communication revolution in general and television in particular as a major weapon in the fight against poverty and illiteracy.

Elaborating on the theme of generating relevant software suited to the country, Dr. Joshi in his Sardar Patel Memorial Lectures, 1985 on 'Communication and Nation Building : Perspective and Policy', observed :

> Relevant software suited to the country can be generated with joint efforts of scientists and media men to introduce the people to the world view of the scientific age and to its fruits which help in solving the age-old and new problems of human life. Equally important is to draw upon the rich software on scientific education from developed countries and to adapt it to the country's needs.

Communication Policies in Five Year Plans

With the beginning of the era of planned development since 1950-51, the role of media came to be emphasized in greater measure. The media was enjoined to provide communication support and inform the general masses about the objectives, targets and benefits of the plans.

The First Five Year Plan was launched in 1951 and the need for communication in support of development was recognized from the very beginning. It was recognized in the official policy :

A wide-spread understanding of the Plan is an essential stage in its fulfilment. An understanding of the priorities which govern the Plan, will enable each person to relate his or her role to the larger purposes of the nation as a whole. All available methods of communication have to be developed and the people approached through the written and spoken word, no less than through radio, film, song and drama. Above all, steps have to be taken to provide literature and information for the people in simple language and on a scale equal to the needs of the country.

The Second Five Year Plan document stressed that the Plan has to be carried into every home in the language and the symbol of the people and expressed in terms of their common needs and problems. It also outlined the measures for expansion of plan publicity through the mass media of communication.

The Third Five Year Plan (1961-66) observed : As part of the programme for strengthening public cooperation and participation during the Third Plan, it is proposed to intensify the existing arrangements for bringing home the implications of rapid development and carrying the message of the Plan to the masses throughout the country.

The observations of two study teams appointed to make proper recommendations : the Study Team on Mass Communication sponsored by the Ford Foundation and the team for the study of plan publicity appointed in 1963, popularly known as the Vidyalankar Committee, are valid even today.

The Ford Foundation Team observed: India's development task is so great and her population so large that only by the most efficient possible programme of public information – necessarily emphasising mass communication – can communicators hope to reach people often enough and effectively enough to activate, on the needed scale, discussion process and subsequent actions in the cities, towns and villages.

The Vidyalankar Committee in its assessment of the results of the efforts of mass media towards creating awareness of the planning process stated : It must be confessed that the needs of the society we have and of the society we are seeking to establish are neither efficiently nor adequately being served by the existing publicity programmes. They have not succeeded in projecting an impressive popular image of the Plans and in inculcating a conception of economic and social development which can be regarded as constituting an integral part of the life and activity of the average citizen. The impact that the existing programmes have created on the public has been tenuous, vague and diffused in an unplanned attempt to achieve too much with too few resources. Plan publicity has failed to touch any section of the population in a forceful manner. Aiming primarily at the dissemination of information, it has lacked purpose and has generally been weak in its approach both in content and the media utilised.

The subsequent plan documents also emphasized different aspects of communication strategy for development. The Fourth Plan document stated : In the spread of information facilities, the imbalance in favour of urban concentrations and prosperous areas continues. There is need for deliberate attempt to inform the people in the rural areas and particularly those in backward regions, about the specific schemes in agriculture, forestry, road construction, marketing, the supply of credit and other inputs so that the benefits of these programmes are more widely spread.

Plan Figures on Broadcasting

(Rs. in lakhs)

	Allocation	Expenditure
Pre-Plan (1948-51)	364.00	–
First Plan (1951-56)	494.00	219.00
Second Plan (1956-61)	800.00	567.00
Third Plan (1961-66)	1400.00	764.00
Three Annual Plans (1-4-1966 to 31-3-1969)	1467.00	1008.00
Fourth Plan (1969-74)	6801.16*	2712.00
	(4510.20 for Sound, 2290.96 for TV)	(1567.00 for Sound, 1145.00 for TV)

*Ceiling for expenditure fixed at Rs. 4000 lakhs.

Source: Akash Bharati. National Broadcasting Trust, Report of the Working Group on Autonomy for Akashvani & Doordarshan, Ministry of Information and Broadcasting, Government of India, New Delhi.

However, from the Sixth Five Year Plan onwards, fund allocation for electronic media and particularly for television progressively increased. The Sixth Plan period (1980-85) saw massive expansion of Indian TV.

The Sixth Plan period with massive investments and phenomenal expansion marks a historical development in the growth and evolution of TV in India.

The objectives of the Seventh Five Year Plan were :

(a) National and emotional integration of various regions of the country,
(b) Utilization of the medium as a means of development and social uplift, and
(c) Dissemination of information and entertainment.

The Plan envisaged the objective of TV reaching the remotest part of the country through a three-tier service : Primary service, National service and Local service.

Today, advancements in information technology and the spread in dissemination of information have virtually become an index of a country's development. Moreover, in a democracy, successful development needs participation of the people which is possible only if they are adequately informed. This calls for optimum investment on collection and dissemination of information and for ensuring access to the media of radio and television. At the same time, these media have to cater to the need for entertainment.

The major thrust of the Seventh Plan relating to Information and Broadcasting sector was on raising the level of consciousness of the people. It laid emphasis on skilful synthesis of traditional and folk forms of communication on one hand and modern audio visual media including satellite communication on the other. The actual outlays and expenditures of different media organisations at the Centre in the Information and Broadcasting sector are as under :

Actual Outlay and Expenditure : Information & Broadcasting Sector

(*Rs. in crores*)

Name of Scheme	Seventh Plan	
	Approved Outlay	Expenditure
Akashvani	700.00	588.20
Doordarshan	700.00	716.07
Films media	41.51	44.32
Information media	30.00	11.45
Total	1471.51	1360.04

By the end of the Seventh Plan, the coverage of Doordarshan had increased to about 53 per cent of the population, the number of its studios had gone upto 31 and the number of transmitters (including transponders) to 535.

Eighth Plan

The thrust of Doordarshan's Plan will consist of consolidation of the achievements by suitably augmenting the production facilities at the existing centres and replacing equipment which has outlived its useful life, extension of coverage to about 76 per cent of the population on completion of all the Eighth Plan schemes and in raising the use of satellite linkage.

During the Eighth Plan, the existing satellite based services will be expanded with main emphasis on introduction of more regional services in the languages of the states through terrestrial rebroadcast transmitters.

Eighth Plan Outlay – Doordarshan

(*Rs. in crores*)

Name of Scheme	Outlay
Continuing Schemes	877.00
Software Scheme and Human Resource Development and Audience Research	200.00
Replacement, Augmentation and Modernisation	270.00
Satellite Services including Regional Services	343.00
Extension of coverage	500.00
Production facilities and other schemes	110.00
Total	2300.00

The Eighth Plan, therefore, visualises an unprecedented growth in terms of extension of coverage, satellite services, software schemes and production facilities.

Implementation of Communication Policies

There has been phenomenal expansion of mass media structures in the country since independence; and more so during the last two decades. Apart from the traditional mass media – print media and the radio – the advent of television and subsequently satellite television, video and now cable television has completely changed the media scenario in the country as never before. The opening up of the Indian media to foreign influences and rapid proliferation of cable television has given rise to the imperative necessity of evolving regulatory mechanism of sorts. Issues like autonomous functioning, accessibility, and software planning for television have been debated and discussed on a large number of occasions and in different fora including the Parliament.

Whereas the electronic media has made significant headway in terms of physical expansion, it leaves much to be desired in terms of software planning, objectivity, implementation of the codes and norms for objective news reporting and above all programmes for development in critical areas like agriculture, health, family welfare, etc. That these communication programmes, as far as their actual implementation is concerned, are not commensurate with the policy recommendations and proposals of large number of media committees is quite evident.

Accessibility and Information Gap

Television remains inaccessible to a majority of people in rural areas, particularly the poor and the backward, for whom the government wants to disseminate developmental and instructional information. Based on a study of 420 villages released by the Audience Research Unit of Doordarshan, it appears only 10 per cent of the rural population (62 crore) is covered by television, as compared to 74.2 per cent of the urban population (22 crore). Thus, the real potential of the rural audience for Doordarshan programmes remains unexplored. Such a situation is bound to accentuate the knowledge gap between the rural and the urban people with serious socio-political implications.

Raising the question : Is television reducing the gap between the Indian urban elites and rural masses, Singhal and Rogers (1989) point out that of the 11 million TV sets in 1988, about three quarters were in four metropolitan cities of Delhi, Calcutta, Madras and Bombay. Television programming decisions are influenced by the elite middle class, who want more entertainment and have less needs for educational programmes than do their rural and urban poor counterparts. This urban bias of commercial television widens the gap between the rich and the poor in India.

In a paper : 'National Cost of Television in India in the Year 2000 : Socio-Economic and Political Implications and Issues, Srivastava (1987) has attempted a profile of population having access to TV in the year 2000, which indicates that the knowledge gap between the poor in urban areas and the rich on the one hand, and between rural and urban people on the other will be accentuated. It will also have serious socio-economic and political implications.

Credibility and Objectivity

Credibility and objectivity of electronic media are the two basic ingredients essential for building up values of trust and reliability between the media and its users. It is more so when the power and reach of the electronic media has increased phenomenonally, thanks to burgeoning expansion of the television network in the country. In order to enforce the values of objectivity and impartiality, various guidelines and codes – The Broadcast Code governing AIR and guidelines for News Policy for Broadcast Media have been made applicable to the AIR and Doordarshan. However, there has been a visible hiatus between what has been prescribed and what is implemented in practice.

The result of the policy of news manipulation over the years has been such that the people are gradually losing faith in the credibility of electronic media and are turning to foreign networks in order to get the true and correct perspective of news and events.

Emphasising the importance of objective and impartial presentation of news, the Verghese Committee observed : The principles of fairness, balance, accuracy and well-rounded objectivity apply not only to news but to all current affairs programmes including commentaries, discussions, news analyses, documentaries, newsreels and magazine features. Balancc, however, does not imply a mechanical balancing of views in each programme, but rather an overall balance achieved over a series of programmes. This is what Akashvani and Doordarshan owe to their audience and this is what the Indian people must always expect of them.

Unfortunately, however, credibility and objectivity continue to be the major casualties, and the misuse of electronic media goes on unabated, codes and guidelines notwithstanding.

In one of its Special Reports on Doordarshan, Hijacking the Medium, *India Today* (15 July 1989) analysed the gaping hole that exists between the precept and practice and as to how objectivity and fairplay are sacrificed at the altar of political gain and expediency. The Special Report gives a blow by blow account of how rules and guidclines are just given a go by in an attempt to cater to the political exigencies of the ruling party.

Development Programmes

The objectives of the television broadcasting include : to provide essential information and knowledge in order to stimulate greater agricultural production, to promote and help preserve environmental and ecological balance, to disseminate message of family planning as a measure of population control and family welfare, to promote national integration, to act as a catalyst for social change, etc. Measured against the above stated objectives, Indian television has come no where near achieving these goals. Instead of working as a change agent, TV has ushered in a phase of consumerism that flaunt a highly westernised life style.

Doordarshan's record in popularising development programmes on agriculture, health, consumer protection, distant education has hardly been a success. A sharper thrust, with the greater and direct involvement and participation of the target groups, in the language and milieu familiar to the viewers would go a long way in popularising these programmes. The observations of the Joshi Committee Report in this context would be particularly relevant. The Committee observed: Communication can also help to convert development programmes into a partnership between the experts and the people. . . . The trouble with many development programmes such as Krishi Darshan is that they are produced within the studio, often with urban men with rural garb. It is often an urban view of rural problems or a view of problems of urbanised villages.

Autonomy

The major underlying reason, for the by and large, lack-luster performance of Doordarshan in not being able to create an impact in the area of nation building activities—as against being an urban medium catering to entertainment primarily, has been lack of freedom for its operational staff. That the government of the day wants to continue using this powerful medium for propagating its political line of thinking is what inhibits it from granting the electronic media an autonomous status. The result is that this promising medium has not been able to develop the characteristics of the national broadcasting service, predominantly Indian in content and character. Instead the impact of the programmes put out by it has been inculcation of western values, alien to the Indian culture, and encouraging consumerism. Lack of autonomy is also responsible, to a large extent, for the medium being not closer to the minds and hearts of the people. Its potential to promote the extension of new knowledge and practices, as an aid to transfer of technology, extension education and social change remains unexplored. An autonomous work culture would certainly have encouraged innovation, diversity of opinions and stimulated national consciousness for the disadvantaged sections of the society.

It is obvious that the objectives for which television was introduced in the country, as a medium for social education, weapon against illiteracy and ignorance, for bringing about awareness among the people of sociological problems, creating sense of participation in India's efforts to usher in a new social order, for playing a vital role in cultivating civic consciousness; remain, by and large, unfulfilled. Television lacks a watch dog mechanism. It is, therefore, important that such an arrangement, which is independent of government control, and could guide and oversee the implementation and enforcement of policy guidelines, is evolved.

These issues are referred to in greater detail in subsequent chapters.

REFERENCES

Akash Bharati : National Broadcast Trust Vol. 1 (1978). Report of the Working Group on Autonomy for Akashvani and Doordarshan, New Delhi : Ministry of Information and Broadcasting, p. 108.

An Indian Personality for TV. Vol. I (1985). Report of the Working Group on Software for Doordarshan, New Delhi : Publications Division, pp. 116-121.

Acharya, R. N. (1987). *Television in India*, New Delhi : Manas Publications, p. 55.

Chawla, N. L. (1982). Communication Policy in India – Software Production and Distribution. *Communicator,* XVII (1) : 2-6, 10.

Chopra, Pran (1986). National Media Policy. *Media Monitor*, pp. 10-11, September-October.

Eighth Five Year Plan (1992-97). Objectives. New Delhi : Planning Commission.

Gupta, V. S. (1983). Indian TV : Software Policy Needed. *Vidura*, 20(5) : 262-265.

Joshi, P. C. (1986). Communication and Nation Building : Perspective and Policy. Sardar Patel Memorial Lectures (1985), New Delhi: Publications Division.

Lee, John A. R. (1976). Towards Realistic Communication Policies : Recent trends and ideas compiled and analysed. UNESCO.

Menon, Narayana (1976). *The Communication Revolution*. New Delhi : National Book Trust, p. 86.

Sen, A.N. (1986). Norms better than broad, rigid terms. *Media Monitor*, May-June, pp. 5-6.

Singhal, Arvind and Rogers, Everett M. (1989). *India's Information Revolution*, New Delhi : Sage.

Srivastava, U. K. (1987). National Cost of Television in India in the year 2000 : Socio-Economic and Political Issues. *Media Asia*, 14(3): 136-144.

UNESCO (1980). Many Voices, One World. The International Commission for the Study of Communication Problems, pp. 40-41.

Winfried, B. Lang (1978). Defining futuristic publicistic aims. *Mass Media Manual*, Friedrich-Ebert-Stiftung, Bonn.

Yadava, J. S. (1994). Communication and Development – The Indian Experience, in Dua, M.R. and Gupta, V.S. (eds.), *Media and Development*, New Delhi : Har Anand Publications.

4

Development Communication : The Shifting Paradigms

The concept of development communication, which has evolved during the last thirty years, does not elicit a question mark any longer. It has achieved a major breakthrough – with substantial amount of thinking going on different aspects – both in theory and in practice.

Development communication constitutes a fascinating subject for more than one reason. It has always engaged and invited a multi-disciplinary approach because of the vastness of the canvas it covers – Development and Communication – both of which have been subject to changing, varying and different meanings and interpretations. It is because both these terms are intimately related to the human society and its affairs in the broadest sense as such. Just as the modern world is confronted with varying levels, stages and standards of development and is divided into Developed and the Developing World, with all its conflicts, controversies and struggles; and communication media it employs to get across the messages – mass media, inter personal, folk, likewise the concept of Development Communication has also been through various paradigms, models and theories. And in the process, it has achieved the distinction of being the subject of several research studies, surveys and analysis – so essential for any subject to receive respectability.

The two components of Development Communication are Development and Communication.

The term Development has been interpreted in various ways by sociologists, economists, development planners, etc. To some it means *Modernisation,* to others *Social Change,* yet to some others it would mean enhancing *Quality of Life* or *Sustainable Development.*

The word 'development' suggests some amount of improvement, self-reliance, uplift and progress; and also self awareness and independence to an extent.

Development has become a catch word and reference to this term has become the order of the day—for politicians and public men, administrators and planners, economists and sociologists. It provides an acid test for the success or the failure of the government of the day. But what does it actually mean. Some of the terms used interchangeably either consciously or unconsciously are : change, growth, progress, modernisation. Likewise, the debate whether development is an objective, process, programme is unending. Economists and social scientists measure development in terms of such abstract indices as gross national product, per capita income and life expectancy, whereas others have stressed the importance of economic impact in accelerating the pace of development, and view development as an all embracing concept, encompassing economic, social, cultural, educational, human face of economic development as well as political aspects of society. Let us examine some of these *concepts of development*.

According to eminent media experts Wilbur Schramm and Daniel Lerner : Development is simply a purposeful change towards a kind of social and economic system that a country decides it wants. The reputed econonist Gunnar Myrdal defines development as "upward movement of the entire social system". However, Prof. Cairncross takes a very broad view of development. 'Development is not just a matter of having plenty of money, nor it is a purely economic phenomenon. It embraces all aspects of social behaviour, the establishment of law and order, the relationships between family, literacy and scrupulousness in business dealings, familiarity with mechanical gadgets on'.

An other scholar of mass communication has suggested the following definition of development : Development in socio-economic terms means improvement in material welfare especially for persons with the lowest income, the eradication of mass poverty and illiteracy alongwith controlling of disease and early death and changes in the composition of inputs and outputs that generally include shifts in the underlying structure of production from agricultural towards industrial activities. In nutshell, it is a process of accelerating the growth with greater social justice aiming at utilizing of resources and opportunities in order to improve the quality of life of the people with special reference to the weaker sections of the society.

Development and Modernization

Modernization is the current term for an old process – the process of social change whereby less developed societies acquire characteristics common to more developed societies. However, this definition of modernization needed to be concretised and the development economists reached the consensus that "growth of output per head of population" was the simple operational definition which provided a comparative measure of achievement level. Modernization is, therefore, the process of social change in which development is the economic component. However, Harold D. Lasswell (1965) pointed out in his paper on, The Sciences of Development, that this transformation in perceiving and achieving wealth-oriented behaviour entails nothing less than the ultimate reshaping and resharing of all social values, such as power, respect, rectitude, affection, well-being, skill and enlightenment. This view of continuous and increasing interaction between economic and non-economic factors in development produced a second step forward, namely, systematic efforts to conceptualize modernization as the contemporary mode of social change that is both general in validity and global in scope.

All models of modernization have dealt in some way with economic development variables : such as industrialization, urbanization, national income and per captia income. The sociologists have added to these variables, an enlightenment variable measured in terms of schooling, literacy and media exposure; political scientists have added a power variable measured in terms of participation and voting, psychologists have added other variables such as empathy and need achievement.

The process of modernization has also taken note of the fact that the process of social change has become the distinctive component of every social system. There remains in the world today few "traditional" social systems that operate with low rates of change over long periods of time. Most societies are in different phases of transition.

It would be interesting to note that empathy – which is a psychic mechanism that enables a person to put himself with a role, time and place different from his own – nourishes the feeling of upward mobility. The mass media which has also been called as mobility mutiplier accelerates the visualisation of well-being among peoples who had never been exposed to the idea that well-being was within their right to demand. Poverty, which was once glorified and accepted as a badge of honour and honesty (eye of the needle philosophy of the Bible) is now rejected as an abject condition unworthy of human acceptance.

An other hall mark of modern society is that of a participant society. This does not, of course, mean that all people must participate continuously in all societal activities. It does mean that enough people must participate continuously in each major institution to make these institutions viable, adaptable and durable.

The process of modernization has been dealt with in some detail because most of the issues of development impinge upon the factors common to both – communication and development.

A widely accepted definition of development was given by Rogers in 'Communication and Development (1976)'. Development, according to Rogers, can be described as : A widely participatory process of directed social change in a society, intended to bring about both social and material advancement (including greater equality, freedom and other valued qualities) for the majority of the people through their gaining greater control over their environment.

Development would mean different things to different people in different countries depending upon the national priorities: One-child family in China, decreased pesticide use in Philippines, creating Computer Culture in Singapore, ORT, clean drinking water and rural roads in India. Development in any particular nation would consist of those projects and programmes which receive top priority in the planning process of that country.

Development and Participatory Democratic Decision-making

Of late, human development or human rights development has also become an important component of the development process. Bella Mody, in her latest publication – *Designing Messages for Development Communication*, has stressed that development would have to include mobilization and reorganization of the marginalized majority to counteract the continued monopolization of all opportunities for growth by a strong minority.

The United Nations Development Program's 1990 analysis of the last three decades of development focuses on a comprehensive view of human development. National development must focus on mobilizing human potential through (a) access to material resources like good health, education, housing, and food, and (b) creation of a culture and environment that guarantees freedom, human rights, and personal self-respect. A participatory approach is essential. The United Nations Economic Commission for Africa and a number of citizen groups which met in Arusha in February 1989 explicitly identified lack of popular participation as the primary cause of Africa's crisis. Overcentralization of power in the state in Africa had constrained the motivation of its people and underutilized their creativity. The failure of governmental organizations to involve the people and meet their needs has led to the steady growth of non-governmental grass root organizations.

Imitation of western mass consumption is not an end in itself or an economically viable option on a global scale since the world's resources cannot sustain such development. Continued monopolization of the benefits of growth by a small proportion (of nations or individuals) is not a politically viable option in the long run. The Dag Hammerskjold Foundation and its Development Dialogue journal have pioneered such an alternative conceptualization which they call Another Development.

The road to development lies in basically grass root participation in decisions on the design and implementation of the particular kind of national transformation desired. The end is to give people's lives back to them—free from domination by colonial powers, an authoritarian state, transnational corporations, and structures of inequality such as caste and class.

We are aware of the latest thinking on what really constitutes development. The World Bank Economist Dr. Mahabub Ul Haq has developed a report on Human Resource Development for different countries of the world. He developed certain measures and indicators to determine the standards of living and growth of human resources. These indicators include expenditure on health, sanitation, education, research and nutrition.

If we look back at different stages, the models of development have undergone changes, we would find that the earliest model had concerned itself with GNP. It had stressed greatly the production aspect. This model was not found satisfactory because it had ignored the distribution aspect of the income and, therefore, the subsequent model concerned itself with Income with Social Justice. Even this model was not considered as a satisfactory and the third model which stressed the quality of life was known as *Overall Quality of Life* (OQL model). This model was also not found to be satisfactory because whereas it stressed the quality of life aspect, it ignored the fact of rapidly dwindling and diminishing natural resources. Therefore, today the latest model on development, stresses *Eco-friendly and Sustainability Nature of Development*. This model stresses the holistic approach which would also combine in itself the elements of morality and ethics.

Human Development Index Model

The Human Development Report for 1994, launched on 1 June this year, underlines resource mobilisation at the global level to provide for basic education, primary health care, safe drinking water and essential family planning services to all people by earmarking at least 20 per cent of the developing countries budgets and 20 per cent of donor aid allocations.

The HDI measures life expectancy, education attainment and income level. It is a composite measure of three basic indicators, namely, human longevity (measured by life expectancy), human knowledge (measured by a combined estimate of adult literacy and mean years of schooling) and standard of living (measured by purchasing power based on per person real gross domestic product which is adjusted for the local cost of living).

The author of the HDI concept, Dr. Haq has stressed : It is time we fashion a new concept of new security, that is reflected in better life for our people, not in battle weapons for our countries. Calling for 3 per cent cut in global military expenditure, with savings diverted to human development programmes, Dr. Haq underlines the necessity of pursuing security through development rather than military expenditure. All these formulations constitute the Agenda for the World Summit on Social Development, which is to be held in Copenhagen in March 1995.

Dr. Haq, who projects a holistic view of human deprivation, and his group of eminent economists and development professionals, proposes an entirely new approach to the development issues : a Global Human Security Fund, an Economic Security Council and a new role for the United Nations and a world social charter. The new proposed model of sustainable development aims at empowerment of people and a new design of development cooperation in accordance with a world social charter.

According to Dr. Haq the global satellite networks have disruptive potential in human societies and his group may even produce a special report on "information systems and human development". Needless to point out that the report on information systems would be as perceptive and stimulating as the yearly UNDP Human Development Report.

The Indian HDI status is 134 in the list of 173 nations, even Pakistan enjoys HDI status at 132, higher than India; most of the Asian countries ranked above India, which means that our performance in terms of life expectancy at birth and educational attainment in terms of adult literacy rate and mean years of schooling did not compare favourably with other Asian neighbours.

To compare favourably with most other countries of Asia and the world there is need to revamp our health and family welfare programmes in terms of enhancing financial resources and policy thrust. Though many spectacular successes have been achieved in the area of health in the country yet there is a long way to go. In spite of our National Health Policy, which reiterates India's commitment to attain health for all by AD 2000, diseases, disability and deaths on account of several communicable diseases are still unacceptably high. Rural health services are still not fully operational. The situation of urban slums is still grave. The Eighth Five Year Plan thrust is in right direction which says that "The Health for All" paradigm must take into account not only high risk vulnerable groups i.e. mothers and children, but must also focus sharply on the underprivileged segments within the vulnerable groups.

The country has made considerable progress in the sphere of education over the past four decades. According to 1991 census, the literacy rate in the country was 52.2 per cent. The literacy rate among females in only 39.3 per cent as against 64.1 per cent for males. It is only 44.2 per cent in rural areas as compared to 73.1 per cent in urban areas and for scheduled castes and scheduled tribes it is 37.4 and 29.6 per cent, respectively. In spite of our considerable progress in education our performance compares unfavourably even among Asian countries. About 19-24 million children in the age group 6-14 and 12 million adult illiterates in the age group 15-35 of which 60 per cent are females are at the bottom rank of our education ladder. No sustainable growth is possible in such a society where vast majority is still illiterate. Therefore, there is urgent need of improvement in education. The major policy package involved relates to increase in budget expenditure on education. The public expenditure on education which is 3 per cent at present should be increased to minimum 6 per cent of the GNP as recommended by NDC and reiterated by the Prime Minister. Such an investment requirement is commensurately high and mobilisation of funds becomes critical consideration.

Even after long years of planned economic development, a substantial proportion of people continues to live below poverty line. Further, the inter-class and inter-regional disparities are increasing. The per capita income of Punjab is 3.30 times more than that of Bihar and 11 states have per capita income lower than national average of Rs. 5529 in 1991-92. It is only Punjab, Haryana, Maharashtra, Gujarat, Andhra Pradesh and Karnataka which have higher per capita income than that of national average. Disaggregating the national income data adjusted for income distribution it has been revealed that HDI in Uttar Pradesh is a third lower than the national average and 60 per cent lower than in Kerala. Similar income disparities exist between rural and urban sectors, and even among these sectors considerable disparities are found among different classes of societies and between male and female. If all these factors are taken into consideration HDI will give an unsatisfactory picture of the economic growth process.

It is, therefore, essential that structural adjustments be introduced for improving the HDI status of India. That is possible only if people's participation is encouraged in the decision-making process and people's organisations are involved in the process.

People's organisations in the form of voluntary organisations and NGOs are becoming popular throughout the world as a countervailing force to the governmental organisations. Such organisations are formed when people of common interest join together. The Seventh and the Eighth Five Year Plans have assigned major role to these organisations.

At present these organisations operate over a wide range of activities, including the anti poverty programmes of the government, training of rural youth, promotion of safe-drinking water, rural housing, promotion of science and technology, health care and family welfare, education, welfare of women and children and programmes for scheduled caste and scheduled tribes. The basic idea of NGO and voluntary organisations is to work for left out classes without any personal gains. They are supposed to do more efficiently the work done by the government or formal organisations. The Government of India appointed a group to suggest improvements in the working of these organisations. The Planning Commission also set up a Task Force to study and develop such organisations. The basic recommendations were :

(i) Greater dissemination of information through newspaper and media,
(ii) Simplified procedures and time-bound disposal of applications for assistance, and
(iii) Preparation of grant-in-aid code and a manual giving details of procedures.

At a time when liberalisation and privatisation are the declared goals of new economic policy, the role of these people's organisations becomes all the more important.

Progress of Nations' Report

In the "Progress of Nations" Report, released by the UNICEF, it has been pointed that atleast 5,000 children die in the country because of malnutrition; 400 being in Rajasthan alone. In NPG rating on child nutrition, India's position is at the very bottom, behind even poorer countries like Bangladesh, Pakistan, Nigeria, etc. An other area where India has lagged behind, is gender equity. The Report notes that India's performance in promoting the status of girls and women remains weak. Whereas India's achievements in the field of immunisation and provision of safe drinking water have been rated as positive, it has to go a long way in eradicating the deficiencies of malnutrition and female illiteracy.

Communication

Communication is the basic instinct of man and a social, economic, political and cultural need. Without communication no society can exist, much less develop and survive. For the existence as well as the organization of every society, communication is a fundamental and vital process. The word *communication* means not only transmission but also *community participation*.

Communication caters to several catcgories of human and social needs, as indicated in the chapter on, 'Communication Policy and Broadcasting" in the Report of the Working Group on Autonomy for Akashvani and Doordarshan:

Social : For the articulation of individual and community needs and aspirations; and for education;

Political : in order to create an informed and enlightened public opinion which is the basis of a democratic society; to create awareness within individuals and within society; to mobilise people behind national policies and programmes;

Economic : as a means of extension and technology transfer; as part of the modernization and development process; and for providing market information as well as for marketing and advertising; and

Cultural : as a means of individual and community expression, discovery and enrichment, and recreation.

Like development, communication has also been a subject matter for various definitions and conceptualisations. However, the basic features of communication are :

(a) Communication is a process for transmission of ideas, thoughts and feelings from one person to another;
(b) Communication is persuasive and seeks to obtain desirable response to what is being transmitted; and
(c) Communication is a two-way process both vertically, and horizontally, in a spirit of 'give and take' or 'send or receive'.

Now naturally the question arises : What is relationship of communication with development *per se*?

According to Wilbur Schramm : Communication is asked to survey a new environment, raise people's aspirations, guide and control a dynamic process, teach new skills and sensitize citizens to a new and different society that is still only in the process of becoming.

Development Communication : Meaning and Nature

Development communication is primarily purposive communication for planned change. It is intended to promote human development which basically means communication that will help reduce poverty, unemployment and social inequality. It is communication with a social conscience.

According to Nora Quebral : Development Communication is the art and science of human communication applied to the speedy transformation of a country and the mass of its people from poverty to a dynamic state of economic growth that makes possible greater social equality and the larger fulfilment of the human potential.

Nora herself is aware of the possibility of refining this definition, even though the basic tenets are unlikely to change (AMIC Study Seminar on Development Communication, 1976).

Although the Development Communication concept has gained recognition during the last few years, it has evolved from the Extension Education discipline introduced in the developing countries in the early fifties. It is significant to point out that the University of Philippines at Los Banos (UPLB) which was the first University in the world to have Development Communication courses, retitled its Master's Degree programme in agricultural communication, as an M.A. in Development Communication. Thus Development Communication is something with which the developing countries are already familiar in different forms like agricultural extension education or rural communication. The origins of Development Communication are, therefore, embedded in the practical efforts and situations of the developing countries in the tasks of changing the life styles, and improving the economic conditions of its people.

Development communication is more than agricultural extension education or rural communication. It does not restrict itself merely to the development of rural areas, nor it is concerned with agricultural development alone. It is oriented towards development – whether it be in rural or urban areas or in agriculture, family planning, nutrition.

Quebral says : The very phrasing of Development Communication indicates its orientation to goals, not to means. Its goals are inherent in the meaning given to development. Some of the more qualitative ones are the enhancement of quality of life, the unfolding of human personality, the humanisation of the individual. *The humanistic goals, as well as the multifaceted nature of development,* (the economic, social, political and cultural aspects) predict a wider scope for the study and practice of Development Communication.

Development Communication – Not Mass Media Manipulation

Development communication embraces the whole gamut of communication media : mass media, interpersonal media and extension agents and other communication change agents. Development communication is not telling people about development programmes, as John Woods, one-time Director of Development Support Communication Services says, which is a part of public relation or public information activity. Just as Development Communication is not public relations job for development, it is not manipulation of mass media either. For mass media tends to be unidirectional, has weak feedback mechanism, is passive and covers an extensive area which percludes effective participation in development process. Since development communication aims at *adaptation and behavioural changes,* it has to be both purposive and persuasive.

The role of mass media in Development Communication will not be those of primary tools, but would only be supportive and in conjunction with ground level change agents whose role would be of central importance. The process of development communication is more personal and has a strong element of human interaction in it. It aims at *motivation and adoption* as against merely *a conveyor of information* which is essentially a function of mass media; and immediate feedback is available through inter personal communication. The interpersonal communication has the advantages of localness, relevance and proximity about them, as have been laid down by Leslie Sargent.

Researches conducted in many developing countries have shown that the mass media, mainly radio and TV are the best communication sources for creating awareness and interest among the audience regarding a new idea or a message. When it comes to adoption process, interpersonal sources such as extension agents, friends, neighbours, local leaders and others are the most effective communication sources. As all these sources are engaged in accomplishing the goals of development, they fall within the ambit of development communication.

Interpersonal Communication

Interpersonal communication is a face-to-face exchange between two or more individuals. The message flow is from one to few individuals, feedback is immediate and plentiful, and the messages are relatively high in socio-emotional content.

The empirical research has revealed that in a democratic society, the mass media are far less potent than had been thought and, in themselves, are quite unable to effect radical changes of opinions, attitudes and actions on subjects that "matter". At the same time one of the major discoveries of research on mass production is the enduring and powerful influencc of interpersonal relations, even in "mass society".

Katz points out in his essay, Diffusion – Interpersonal influence, that at first interpersonal influence seemed irrelevant to the students of the media of mass communication. Later on several studies were conducted on the influence of different channels of communication. Taken together, these studies suggested that *conversation with other people* is generally more influential than the mass media in decisions to accept some new idea or practice; that people who influence others are typically close associates.

Rural sociologists and others have found that the channel that makes for awareness of an innovation is typically a formal one – generally one of the mass media, or an institutionalised source such as a dealer or a salesman, whose job is to spread news of the innovation as quickly as possible to as many people as possible. But extremely few people adopt an innovation on the basis of awareness alone.

The mass media, "inform" decisions; interpersonal contacts "support" and "legitimate" them. Interpersonal influence is a two-way communication, the audience can talk back and convince itself. It is flexible, it is more trust worthy. If a goal of interpersonal communication is to achieve a changed attitude to this end, as a rule, interpersonal communication is more effective than mass communication. Development communication emphasises invariably the results, a response to a message transmitted. It is the *quality of response* that provides the acid test and constitutes one of the salient features of development communication.

Paradigms of Development Communication

A paradigm is a mental model that seeks to explain a phenomenon. During 1960s, the main paradigm about development guided many development programmes. The *dominant paradigm of development* stressed economic growth (measured as annual rate of growth in a nation's GNP) through industrialization. At the heart of industrialization were inputs of *technology* and *capital* which substitute labour. Heavy industries like steel mills and hydro-electric dams were imported from industrialised countries. Mass communication was considered a powerful, direct force for development. The influential works of Lerner and Schramm led communication scholars to expect mass media to be a "magic multiplier" of development. Administrators, researchers and field workers sincerely believed in the great power of mass media as harbingers of modernizing influences. Lerner saw dynamics of social development as : a nucleus of mobile, change-accepting personalities, a growing mass media system to spread ideas of social mobility and change, urbanization, literacy and industrialization, higher per capita income and political participation.

The above paradigm of development started to break down in early seventies. It became increasingly clear that the role of mass communication in facilitating development was only limited and indirect. The dominant paradigm of development took a very negative view of tradition. This notion does not have too many supporters in recent times. The dominant paradigm was found wanting in several respects. It was criticized for :

(i) defining development only in terms of certain quantifiable characteristics such as GNP, and per capita income;
(ii) for encouraging capital intensive techniques in capital poor developing nations and neglecting labour intensive strategies;
(iii) focusing only on constraints to development that existed within a developing nation and largely ignoring constraints that were imposed from outside; and
(iv) supporting a top down approach to planning and development.

This approach did not reflect the new concern for self-reliance and popular participation in development activities.

New Development Paradigm

The fall of the dominant paradigm caused considerable academic rethinking about development. The dominant paradigm was giving way to a 'new' paradigm for development.

This new paradigm was pluralistic in that it recognized many pathways to development. It was also less western in its cultural assumptions. Key elements in the new development paradigm include :

1. Greater equality in the distribution of development investment, information and the consequent socio-economic benefits of focusing on such weaker sections of the population as the poor, women and racial and ethnic minorities.
2. Popular participation, knowledge sharing, and empowerment to facilitate self-development efforts by individuals, groups and communities.
3. Self-reliance and independence in development, emphasizing the potential of local resources. Self-reliance became a key concept at both the national and local levels, implying that every nation and perhaps every village, could develop in its own way.
4. Integration of traditional and modern communication systems and the use of 'little media' alongwith the 'big media' of television and film, in order to facilitate development.

The new paradigm of development was a framework in which communication played a facilitative role in development. Self-development approaches to development communication led to more popular participation, mass mobilization, and group efficacy, with greater responsibility for development planning and execution at the local level. The main roles of mass communication in such self-development are : to provide technical information about development problems and possibilities, and about appropriate innovations; and to circulate widely information about self-development accomplishments by local groups so that other such groups could profit from others' experiences.

Development Communication in the Indian Context

Evolving a development communication plan for India in reality means paying attention to local and sub-regional strategies. The real problem in one of tailoring the media to suit the aspirations of the people and mobilising media for development keeping in view that illiteracy is the main barrier to communication.

Development journalism in India made its debut in 1950s as a result of launching of several development oriented projects through Five Year Plans. There have been several innovative development journalism programmes in the country, the most memorable being the series of articles and features, *Our Village Chhatera,* in the *Hindustan Times* under the leadership of the doyen of Indian journalists—B. G. Verghese. This series blazed a new trail in the area of development journalism and elicited attention due to the freshness and novelty of approach and the interest it had created in the rural problems of the area. Several other outstanding examples in the areas of Rural Press and Rural Reporting could also be legitimately categorised as Development Journalism. Wilbur Schramm, in his book, *Mass Media and National Development,* considered rural press as one of the great movers of national development.

It has been widely accepted that so long as the rural population does not possess information processing capacity to use opportunities made available by the government, the massive economic inputs notwithstanding, the fruits of planned development will not reach the poor, those living below the poverty line and whose economic status the government plans profess to improve. The Rural Press is remarkably suited to fill in this missing link between the development functions and the users and consumers of development information.

Satellite Instructional Television Experiment (SITE)

There has been a major shift in the developmental approach to communication since 1970 when the planners realised the need to give priority to communicating with the rural masses. SITE (August

1, 1975 to July 31, 1976) was the first major investment that demanded overall planning and execution of a communication plan through an electronic medium the sole beneficiaries of which were the rural population of 2,400 villages spread over six States. The SITE Programme was aimed at promoting through the audio-visual medium skills useful to the farmers as well as instilling in them the habits of healthy living; to make them aware of the process of modernisation of life and society. It also aimed at supplementing school children curriculum through non-formal means of conveying information.

It was for the first time that an effort was made at a heavy investment to bring the message of modernisation to the rural folks. The SITE objectives included the testing of the value of satellite technology in the rapid development of effective mass communication in developing countries.

Some of the major benefits of SITE programme were that the rural population was directly exposed to government plans and policies without the normal channels of distortion due to hierarchical functionaries. There was a marked increase in awareness of the rural population of the right to minimum wages, land for house building for the landless, need for immunisation against diseases, need to purify drinking water and certain other farming and nutritional practices. They also became aware of the different cultures, traditions and customs of many states in India and gained an overall view of what this subcontinent stands for.

Social Marketing and Social Mobilisation

Social marketing, which is essentially the use of marketing principles and techniques to promote concepts and products for the purpose of social change, is one of the newly emerging communication planning strategies. This approach has been successfully put in practice in the implementation of various projects in Third World countries on social issues like immunisation, literacy, planning for health and nutrition-oriented public education campaigns.

Allen (1990) has explained the concept in some detail as under :

Social marketing is the use of marketing principles and techniques to "self" concepts or products for the purpose of social change. In the case of education, selling the concept of parental involvement in education is based on the assumption that the involvement will contribute to the public good. Some social marketing schemes create products, such as maths work books for parents to use at home with their children or radio programmes focused on school issues. Typically, these products are subsidized to ensure that the cost to the consumer is low enough so as not to inhibit their use. However, social marketers believe that the actual sale, rather than the free distribution of the product is important because it helps to ensure consumer motivation by forcing people to pay for the product and thereby contributes to long term self-sufficiency of the education project.

Essential to a social marketing programme is the need to understand the consumer or target audience. All four elements, product, price, place and promotion, assume that the social marketer has taken the time to understand the needs of the target audience and what might motivate them to subscribe to a concept or product. Marketing places emphasis on the consumer's needs, attitudes, constraints and opportunities.

Social marketing projects need to be handled professionally and systematically which would include : Programme analysis, audience analysis, setting objectives, developing a strategy and also a Plan of Action. It has been stressed that social marketing projects, in order to be successful, must focus on a well segmented target to maximize impact of message.

Ray (1987) outlines the successful social marketing strategy evolved for rice promotion campaign in the Philippines : Evidence indicates that combining some of the social marketing techniques learned from the health sector with some mass marketing techniques used in previous agricultural projects could help agricultural extension programmes to : cover the target audience comprehensively and quickly, be flexible in recommending technology packages, gather information from farmers as a basis for adopting recommendations, and collaborate with researchers, suppliers and marketing service.

From experiences in health and agriculture extension, three elements appear to be vital for success in communicating with farmers – farmer orientation, targeted change, and an integrated media metwork. Agricultural communicators must learn when addressing farmers, to use a vocabulary that presents issues and problems from the farmer's orientation.

Targeted change means information must reach the farmer when he needs it, and often, in order to reinforce a new behaviour so it becomes part of his routine practice. This calls for a comprehensive communication strategy that accounts for the many unpredictable factors farmers confront throughout a production cycle.

The third part of this social marketing package is the media network. Elements of each of the media groups (broadcast, print, interpersonal) must be selected carefully and then integrated in a way that builds upon their unique advantages so that a multiplier effect is achieved. This can be accomplished by using channel strategies that are based on pre-programme research to determine where and how people get information.

Organized effectively around these three elements, communication can directly increase programme participation. It can also provide information to reduce risk and improve efficiency in using services and lead to the adoption of new practices.

Social mobilization has been defined by UNICEF as the planned process of enlisting the support and active involvement of all sectors within a society that can play a role in achieving an agreed social objective, converging the interest and actions of institutions, groups and communities towards the objective, thereby mobilizing the human and material resources to reach it, and rooting it in society's and the community's conscience to ensure its sustainability.

A series of three training workshops on information, education and communication planning for health and nutrition conducted by AMIC from 1987-1989, developed a package comprising eight modules in Public Education and Social Marketing. These modules were adapted by women leaders for local training purposes and later assessment from the field indicated positive response to the material.

Development Support Communication – FAO Expert Consultation

The FAO has been doing pioneering work in the area of communication for development. It has developed several case studies and success stories whereby communication was successfully used for development purposes in developing countries. The Report of FAO Expert Consultation on DSC held in 1987 stated as under :

1. Although it started out with a strong emphasis on the use of media, development communication is seen today more as a social process designed to seek a common understanding, or consensus, among all the participants of a development initiative, so creating a

basis for concerted action. And the media are now seen as useful tools to help bring about this process, and to assist in learning. Their use is not an end in itself, and interpersonal communication plays a major role.

2. By shifting the emphasis away from the top-down approach and working instead on knowledge-sharing to allow people to make informed decisions concerning adoption, adaptation, or even rejection of innovations, communication can :

- Create situations conducive both to the sharing of knowledge and to the participation of people in situation analysis, development planning and management, and decision making. Participation is the *sine qua non* of development.
- Spread knowledge of mutually decided proposals to the rural populace.
- Motivate people to take appropriate collective action using interpersonal approaches, group action and multi-media campaigns.

3. Development communication is a broad-based system for which the primary requirement is communication know-how rather than agricultural know-how. It covers a wide spectrum of the factors involved in development : situation analysis, the involvement of people in the planning and implementation of development activities, motivation, behavioural change, and education and training methods. Communication can, and should be, applied to helping people bring about improvements in all aspects of rural life, not just agriculture.

Lessons from Grameen Bank, Bangladesh

This case study is a remarkable example of the successful use of communication in support of development. This case study underlies the value and importance of *shared interests, credibility and trust.*

The economy of Bangladesh, which has one of the highest population densities in the world, is characterized by poverty, negation of farm labour and women, accompanied by a pervasive devaluation of women. It was for providing relief to this section of the poorest of the poor section of the society that the Grameen Bank Project was taken up with the following objectives :

1. to extend credit to the landless poor, men and women;
2. to eleminate the exploitation of the money lenders;
3. to create opportunities for self-employment among those vast, but underutilized human resources; and
4. to bring the poor within the fold of some organizational format which they can operate for mutual support and benefit.

This project adopted certain innovative methods of group meetings, centre meetings and open conduct in front of the members. The members developed confidence to speak up and learn to be proud of improved assets through their own work. The members took great pride in being honourable and making their payment on time. The message that the Grameen Bank has given to the members is : *You must go forward together and help each other.*

The National Workshop of 100 Women Centre Chiefs adopted a social development constitution of the Grameen Bank. The underlying philosophy of the working is Communication is participation.

Bank workers and social development officers have very few communication media at their disposal for centre meetings or workshop sessions. There are no slide or film projectors, no video equipment and rarely a poster. Meetings are taking place in remote community halls without electricity. But human ingenuity can solve such a problem. The Bank has introduced innovation in visual aids. Small picture cards 10 × 15 cm are handed out to the women so each participant can tangibly hold the topic of discussion in front of her. After use, the cards are collected ready for use in another meeting. It works beautifully and it could not be simpler and cheaper. The Bank has decided that the time has come for trying video in its training programmes and, characteristically staff members themselves will learn by trial and error whether it is worth it.

The grass root system for making small loans available to the poor has taken root and blossomed in the Bangladesh countryside. And this concept, in similar grass root fashion, has extended beyond the borders of this tiny, overpopulated country rife with poverty. This way of fighting poverty has been implemented in some 30 countries around the world and about 40 funds in the United States are modelled on the Grameen Bank, whose symbol is a green house.

Modelled on the Grameen Bank, other non-governmental

organisations have emerged in big cities to fill the gap. The Shakti Foundation for disadvantaged women initiated the Urban Credit Programme in April 1992 for squatters and women living in slums, in urban areas. Shakti's objectives include providing credit for income generating activities to encourage savings and to provide training in skill development.

There would certainly be many more such case studies and success stories of imaginative exploitation of Development Communication in several countries.

Developmental Slots not imaginative

However, the state of affairs about Development Communication in India could be best described in the words of the Minister for Information and Broadcasting, who while addressing the professional body of communication experts on 12 June 1993 said that programmes on socio-economic developmental issues produced by All India Radio and Doordarshan had failed to fascinate listeners and viewers. He observed: No matter the amount of money spent or the time allotted to the media some of the programmes are dull and do not have any imagination or concern for the client, the minister said expressing concern at the quality of radio and TV programmes on developmental issues. As the various types of programmes oriented on socio-economic development issues are not imaginative and fascinating, the listener or the viewer simply turns off the knob, as a result the developmental measures do not percolate to the people.

Let us for once hope that the government pronouncements are translated into action.

REFERENCES

Akash Bharati : National Broadcast Trust (1978). Report of the Working Group on Autonomy for Akashvani and Doordarshan, New Delhi : Ministry of Information and Broadcasting.

Allen, D. H. (1990). A Primer on Social Marketing. *Development Communication Report,* 2(69) : 7.

An Indian Personality for Television (1985). Report of the Working Group of Software for Doordarshan, New Delhi : Publications Division, pp. 144-124.

Baru, Sanjaya (1994). The Development Mirror—The HDR's Gauntlet to Governments. *Times of India,* 8 June.

Berriegan, Frances J. (1977). A manual on mass media in population and development. UNESCO.

Braid, F. R. (1993). Communication and development in the new Asian context. *AMCB*, 23(4) : 10-11.

Chamola, S. D. (1994). Human Development – The Missing Link in Indian Economic Development. Presidential Address in the 14th Annual Conference of the Haryana Economic Association, 19-20 March.

Elgarbi, Ali Z. (1987). Pathways to development. *Media Asia,* 14(3) : 130-34.

FAO (1987). The paradigm of communication in development : From knowledge transfer to community participation – Lessons from the Grameen Bank, Bangladesh. Development Communication – A Case Study, Rome.

FAO (1987). Development Support Communication Expert Consultation, Rome.

Forsythe, Victor and C. Chu Godwin (1988). Thirty years of research into relationship between communication and development have not been able to fully explain this complex social process. *Media Asia*, 15(2) : 90.

Gamma (1994). Banks for the poor, ideas for the rich. *The Hindu,* 15 May.

Gupta, V. S. (1979). Development communication – An emerging concept. *Vidura*, 16(3) : 197-199.

Guru, B. P., Mahesh Chandra and Puttaraju, K. (1993). The language journalism education as an instrument of development : An Indian perpective. National Seminar on Current Trends in Journalism and Communication Education in Indian Languages, Hyderabad.

Guy, de Fontagalland (ed.) (1976). AMIC Study Seminar on Development Communication , March 1985 – A Report, AMIC, Singapore.

Habermann, Pater and Guy de Fontgalland (1978). Development Communication. AMIC, Singapore.

Katz, Elihu (1968). Diffusion : Interpersonal influence. *International Encyclopaedia of Social Sciences,* pp. 178-184. The Macmillan Company and The Free Press.

Kunczik, Michael (1984). Communication and social change. Friedrich-Ebert-Stiftung, Bonn.

Lerner, Daniel (1968). Modernisation : Social Aspects. *International Encyclopaedia of Social Sciences,* pp. 386-396. The Macmillan Company and The Free Press.

Melkote, Srinivas R. (1991). *Communication for development in the third world—Theory and practice,* New Delhi : Sage.

Mody, Bella (1991) *Designing messages for development communication*, New Delhi : Sage.

Ray, Howard, E. (1987) Communicating with farmers : Lessons learned and to be learned : *Development Communication Report,* 3(58) : 1-2.

Sedere, U. Mohittige (1991). Second Cycle Development Problems and the Role of Adult Education – A Case Study of Sri Lanka. ASPBAE Courier No. 52, Canberra : Asian South Pacific Bureau of Adult Education.

Singhal, Arvind and Rogers, Everett M. (1989). *India's Information Revolution*, New Delhi : Sage.

Tiwari, I. P. (1987) Communication, Technology and Development, New Delhi: Publications Division.

Ward, W .B. (1971). Mass Media in India's Agricultural Development, *Vidura*, 5.

5

Rural Development and Media Strategies

India is predominantly a rural country – a land of villages. Notwithstanding the rapid industrial and technological progress made by India since independence, the Indian economy is basically agricultural. A little over one-third of the country's national income is derived from agriculture and allied activities, which absorbs about two-thirds of its working force. According to the 1991 census, out of the total population of over 900 million, the rural population accounted for 76.69 per cent; the urban figure being 23.31 per cent. The urban-rural distribution pattern indicates that India continues to be mainly a rural country although her urban population has increased by nearly 50 millions during the last decade.

Statistics apart, the cultural ethos and milieu of India is rural. The Indian fairs and festivals are organised to celebrate the bountiful gift of nature – coinciding with the two crop cycles – *rabi* and *kharif*. An average Indian farmer is a hard working, honest and sincere person deeply attached to his fields. The rural areas are repositories of rich cultural heritage. The Indian tradition of dance and music – the exuberance of *Bhangra* of Panjab or the grace of *Bihu* dance of Assam – have strong rural roots. Not only this, the objectives of planned economic development since 1952, the beginning of the planning era have been to ensure that rural areas are provided viable means of economic growth.

All this should have made the rural areas of India bustling with prosperity. The rural scenario, however, is not that optimistic. A large majority of villages do not get even a newspaper or a magazine. There are virtually no retail outlets for books, magazines or newspapers in rural areas. The library system, which, in any case, is poor even in towns, does not exist in villages. As such the rural reading habit does not exist. The literacy percentage in rural areas is low. While the total number of literates has increased four-fold in thirty years; simultaneously, the total number of illiterates has increased from 300.9 millions in 1951 to 437.63 million illiterates in 1981, of which 84.4 per cent live in rural areas. This number has further increased in 1991 census. No wonder, the exposure of villages to literacy and consequently to the press has been so poor. The percentage of population in villages living below the poverty line is about 40 per cent. The dismal situation exists in spite of the massive efforts undertaken by the government to ameliorate the conditions of rural poverty ever since the beginning of planned economic development since early fifties.

Rural Development

Rural development, in the broad sense of the term, holds the key to all economic progress, industrial or agrarian, urban or rural. The World Bank Rural Development Policy Sector Study of 1975 defines rural development as :

> Rural development is a strategy designed to improve the economic and social life of a specific group of people – the rural poor – and involves extending the benefits of development to the poorest among those who seek a livelihood in rural areas.

According to Saha *et al.* (1978), it involves :

1. Physical development : communication, transport, sewage, irrigation, energy, forestry, animal conservation, environment;
2. Economic development : agriculture, business, industry;
3. Social development : education, culture, sports, political activities; and
4. Health development : nutrition, sanitation, community health, prevention of water and air pollution.

A large number of schemes and programmes, notable amongst them being IRDP, TRYSEM, FFW, DPAP and DDP were launched primarily to improve the living standards of the mass of low income population.

Regarding the effect of rural development, Dutt (1990) has pointed out: Rural development, has had the effect of increasing income disparities, even though by a process of trickling down it improves somewhat the standard of living of the poor, has dangerous potentials. The discontent caused thereby, and by the lack of social security which often accompanies income disparities, frequently manifests itself in undesirable channels such as religious fundamentalism, regional chauvinism and even secessionism.

According to Kamta Prasad (1990), the approach to rural development followed so far has been essentially bureaucratic rather than participatory. Rural development plans have been prepared at the national and state headquarters and passed on to local level offices of the government for execution. Involvement of the local people has been rather limited. Consequently, there has often been a mismatch between what the people wanted and what they got from the Government. Whether it is IRDP, DPAP or any other programme, the dead uniformity which has occurred in the name of national planning has proved highly unproductive. As Sardar Tarlok Singh has pointed out, the interest at the higher level has been increasingly to get at quick numerical results which are easy to report, add up and publicise in one form or another with too little attention to the true impact on the conditions of the poeple.

In his eminently readable monograph, Development Theories – NGOs and Self Help Organizations, Bongartz (1993) has analysed as to what went wrong with the rural development approaches :

> Actually, the community development approach did not provide much support to self-help activities at the village level. Decisions were still made in the centralized planning apparatus. The bulk of the input provided to the villages was absorbed by the better off sections of the rural communities. Existing power structures were accepted and not much was done to set up local self-help organizations of the poor. Therefore, in terms of poverty alleviation or eradication of problems, not much progress could be reported.

There is also increasing recognition that past development efforts had not fully taken into account social and community needs, cultural values and capabilities as key elements in rural development programmes. However, now there is belated realization that the needs of the people should be at the core of the development process which should be driven by social and environmental concerns rather than economic considerations alone.

In the subsequent Five Year Plans, the Planning Commission observed : What matters is not the precise increase in national product that is achieved in five or ten years, but whether we can assure, within a specified time frame, a measurable increase in the welfare of the millions of the poor.

It is now accepted that rural development should mean not only an increase in the per capita GNP but greater equality in its composition. This would involve greater emphasis on social services like health, education, family welfare to the poor.

There is also renewed emphasis on people's participation in development programmes. According to Kamta Prasad (1990) : Involvement of the local people in schemes of rural development is expected to result in better planning and decision-making because the local people have a better awareness of their needs and preferences and fuller information on the conditions and possibilities of their areas. The local communities, with a more intimate knowledge of the inter-dependence of activities at the micro level, would be in a better position to develop integrated programmes which would avoid a duplication and produce the maximum impact with minimum cost.

Many development thinkers and agencies are becoming increasingly determined that people's needs and demands are more fully understood, and wherever appropriate, integrated into wider development context.

Media strategies for rural development will have to be essentially geared to the ethos and relevance to the people whom development plans are indented to benefit. The basis of these media strategies should highlight the localness of approach and dissemination of culturally appropriate and user friendly technology. Ramanamma (1993) has pointed out :

> There is a general assumption on the part of media professionals that they can disseminate a particular idea without a dialogue with the grass root people because they consider themselves as 'specialists'. A majority of them show little or no respect for the experience and knowledge of the

people – the creative potential of the peasants or slum dwellers. They fail to understand that poor people are more suited to depict the issues concerning them and present their own lives. In order to achieve participation, consultation, cooperation, and effective mobilization of people, the media system would need to assist in establishing a sense of community and would need a desire to resolve the issues concerning them.

The media strategies would succeed in creating the right kind of climate and environment for development only within the parameters and constraints which are associated with the rural population. These strategies would have to be innovative, realistic, chiselled and shaped to fine tune the aspirations of the people; and should preferably be operated by the local resource persons in tune with the sensibilities of the clientele.

Rural Press

The rural press, as a medium for community communication, with its potential for creating awareness of, and articulating people's problems; as a link between the policy-makers, development bureaucracy and farmers; as a second line of conversion of scientific knowledge into information for utilization in the field situation, imparting adult education and also as a vehicle for reinforcing the literacy habit; is being increasingly recognised as an important and viable means for the promotion of social awareness and national development. Rural press is a promising medium for disseminating information and knowledge about nutrition, health and hygiene, improved farm practices, family planning measures and development plans to those sections of the society where the information is needed most. Special attention has been paid to its problems, prospects and promotion by several organisations such as, UNESCO (which had launched a project for encouraging the rural press in Africa in the early seventies), IPDC, and other UN agencies under the programme of DSC. The growing interest in the rural press by these organisations and now even by newspapers published from metropolitan centres, augurs well and testifies to the important role that the rural press can play as an integral part of the rural communication development process.

The IRPA defines a rural paper as one which devotes at least 40 per cent of its editorial space to agriculture, horticulture, community development, cooperation and Panchayati Raj, etc. A rural paper would essentially be a language paper published from outside the metropolitan and big cities and most probably from district headquarters. It is essentially a small newspaper, which as per the classification of the RNI will primarily have a circulation below 15,000 copies. It caters to local issues of immediate importance to the people. According to another definition, a rural newspaper is one that is primarily published from a rural area, devoting at least 50 per cent of its contents to the problems relating to the rural community, in a language akin to the idiom of the rural readers.

The community newspapers by definition are the papers located outside the capital and their focus is more on local news.

The Regional Press with its grassroot contacts through a network of correspondents in district towns, touching upon local issues and topical subjects relevant to the common man, concerning his everyday life and written in a style close to his mind and heart, enjoys a large measure of similarity with the rural press as far as language, local interest and subject spread is concerned. Some regional newspapers brought out from bigger towns have large circulations and multi editions.

The rural press, therefore, shares most of the characteristics of the community newspapers, local newspapers and the regional press. Several experts on the subject have, therefore, been using these terms interchangeably, notwithstanding certain differences in their circulation, subject spread, etc. Some of the regional papers, may, for instance, have a larger circulation and cover a vast range of topics from sports to national politics, etc. In such cases it would perhaps be too far fetched to classify these papers as the rural press. The following statement may, therefore, generally be the most acceptable concept of the rural press:

> When we refer to the rural press we mean small newspapers with small circulations, serving small communities and catering to their special needs and interests, that cannot be met by the urban press.

Role of Rural Press

Wilbur Schramm, in his book, *Mass Media and National Development*, considered rural newspapers as one of the great movers of national development. Such a newspaper gives the neo-literate reason to learn to read better and makes public participation in governmental policies more informed, relevant and meaningful. Apart from broadening the actual educational base of its readers, the rural papers break down the barriers of isolation and provide written material to the villagers who have learnt to read so that they can apply their reading ability to increase their production.

The printed word, particularly in the rural areas, has a fascination of its own. It is a catalyst of change and growth. To improve the recognition, understanding and appreciation of the printed word, specially for those for whom it is not a routine matter, to interact with books and newspapers, is a worthwhile task. Aldous Huxley has said : Every man who knows how to read has the capacity to magnify himself, to multiply the way in which he exists, to make his life full, significant and interesting.

The rural newspaper, with its simple language and contents closest to the interest of its readers, reinforces this reading habit, day in and day out. Since reading is basic to the understanding of the working of a host of social; economic and political institutions, the rural press by cultivating and reinforcing the reading habit, performs an important role in enhancing social and political awareness.

The International Commission for the Study of Communication Problems, while summarising its recommendations says : The development of a community press in rural areas and small towns would not only provide print support for economic and social extension activities. This would also facilitate the production of functional literature for neo-literates as well.

In a seminar on Publishing for Rural Areas in developing countries, the well known sociologist Rajni Kothari (1981) was quoted as under : Acquisition of a minimum education level greatly raises a person's skill and his capacity to enter the employment market; it also raises his sense of potency and his ability to relate himself to the outside world, his sense of political efficacy, and his general self-confidence and sense of dignity.

If the rural press were to serve its function of reinforcing literacy or preventing readers from lapsing into illiteracy once again, it would have fulfilled a task of great national importance and particularly so, in developing countries where illiteracy continues to be a serious problem.

The importance of rural press has been underlined in the famous treatise, Communication and Change in the Developing Countries, one of the pioneering efforts focusing on the above subject. Nair (1967) has stated :

> Sometimes it has been asked whether the host of small district newspapers which have come out in recent years serve any useful purpose. They are said to confine their attention mainly to local complaints and disputes. I have regarded these district papers as of immense value, for they focus the attention of the local population on local development effort and assist in creating interest in the local affairs. I personally know of a number of cases in which these small newspapers have exercised considerable influence on local administration and have helped to build local opinion on political and economic issues. If development requires local participation, these district papers have to play an important role in mobilizing local effort. It may be conceded that all of them are not motivated by the highest ideals, and some of them may be instruments of local politicians, but as a whole they are of great assistance to local development. Political decentralization and establishment of Panchayati Raj have created a new political structure in local administration. The Zila Parishads and Panchayat Samitis have been entrusted with wide powers in the spheres of local administration and local development. The small district newspapers have the same significance in local affairs as provincial papers in state matters and metropolitan papers in national problems. The study team on Five Year Plan publicity has described this section of the press as the most important link in the communication chain. There can be little doubt of what a healthy mofussil Press can do to inculcate high ideals of public service and a sense of dedication to people's weal and welfare in the making of the local self-governing institutions.

A rural newspaper provides a forum to articulate the urges of the common man. It takes up local issues and immediate requirements, affecting the people. It gives greater importance to the problems agitating the ordinary people : unemployment, scarcity of agricultural inputs, the law and order situation at the village level, etc. It is best suited to act as the second level of conversion of scientific knowledge into information in a usable form for the benefit of the ultimate clientele – the farmers.

It is well recognised that, by and large, the first conversion of scientific knowledge into information takes place at the level of research institutions. Literature produced at this stage for common consumption can be utilised by the educated and high level functionaries having access to such literature. Such information is further converted, for the second time, in the form of newspapers, pamphlets, newsletters and magazines, and transferred through the government extension agencies to the lower level government functionaries like the VLWs or the ADOs. It is here that the rural press plays perhaps its most important role. This role is, in fact, the primary role that most of the rural extension papers and magazines brought out by the agricultural universities and state departments of agriculture are performing. In the absence of the rural press, the knowledge generated in the experimental fields and laboratories of research institutions and universities would have remained confined to the files of the researchers and scientists.

Source of Development Information

It is not only with respect to the scientific knowledge that the rural press works as the second level of conversion. It also plays an important role as conveyor of information about development plans and programmes of the government such as availability of seeds and fertilizers and loans through the banks and the cooperative societies, market rates of agricultural produce, etc. It establishes a link between government functionaries and the village and fills the much needed gap in the information process. It has been widely accepted that so long as the rural population does not possess information processing capacity to use opportunities made available by the government, the massive economic inputs notwithstanding, the fruits of planned development will not reach the poor, those living below the poverty line and whose economic status the government plans profess to improve. The rural press is remarkably suited to fill in this missing link between the development functions and the users and consumers of development information.

The rural press is also expected to, and in many cases, does perform the role of a crusader on behalf of its readers. The well known rural journalist, G. P. Jain, has written about the Rural Press in Seminar in its issue on 'The Village and the Communicator' :

> A rural paper, I can speak from my 25 years experience, will have a great and loyal readership, if it can also fight for its readers. Not a day passes without an injustice being perpetrated on a village community by the rich few or the underlings of bureaucracy. Like a social worker, a rural paper can win the people's confidence and trust if it takes up their causes in a crusading spirit. What the urban press did during the independence struggle for the national cause, the rural press can do now for the rural communitics and earn their great gratitude.

A similar role for the rural press – that of reporting injustice being done to the people living in villages under the tyranny of the rich and the powerful was pointed out by another eminent journalist, D. R. Mankekar who said that crime unreported was crime licenced and encouraged and, therefore, it would be the duty of the papers working in rural areas to expose such injustice to the people.

According to a UNESCO study on rural newspapers in Africa, the rural press ensures a dialogue between rural environment and urban environment.

A significant feature of the rural press is its closer identity with the people on account of emotional and linguistic affinity. The English language newspapers are more analytical in their approach and are interested in broader subjects like functioning of international institutions, legislative reforms, separation of the judiciary from the executive, economic reforms, etc. They do not articulate the urges of the common man; whereas the editors of rural or district newspapers give greater importance to the problems concerning the common man – unemployment, rising prices, law and order difficulties at the local level, etc. The rural newspapers, which are in contact with the grassroots levels, and are aware of local problems, will be able to communicate in the language and idiom that the people understand.

The rural newspaper is in touch with the day-to-day life

problems of the common man – a small scale or marginal farmer, rural artisan, village school teacher. The literature and information produced by the rural press – profile of an artisan, success story of a progressive farmer, problems faced in the marketing of agricultural produce, social superstitions and taboos inhibiting economic growth and productivity – not only reflect the life in the villages, but also provide a different perspective and frame of reference for planners and policy makers. The feedback so available would be of great help for reorienting development plans. Like the local radio stations, the rural press also serves as the source of information about various schemes, plans, projects and facilities available like credit, seed, fertilizer.

The rural press evolves its own editorial and news structure as also its own vocabulary. As to the resource personnel, it generally has school teachers, community development workers, agricultural extenstion workers and the local legislator as writers and contributors. Written in the simple, regional language of the area, the rural press is ideally suited to be a "People's Forum" through which people's grievances may be conveyed to the authorities in the district. It will, thus, encourage a two-way flow of information, rather than being unidirectional which most of the mass media is at present.

Rural newspapers are the most suitable medium for localised programming. Through locally produced news and commentaries, feature articles, interviews, pictures, stories and letters to the editor, the newspaper can stir up interest, initiate discussion and serve as a sounding board for audience reaction.

According to the research findings on Agricultural Journalism and Rural Development in the Research Bulletin No. 35, brought out by the Division of Agricultural Extension, IARI : the question of effectiveness of content is linked with the background of writers who contribute articles to farm periodicals. On the whole, readers have attached more authenticity to scientists and extension workers. However, readers regarded the articles written by them to be too scientific and technical in nature. Thus, there is a need to have scientists and extension workers as writers who could write without the theoretical bias and have a first hand knowledge of field problems. Then will have to acquire techniques of writing technical articles in simple language by using local equivalents for technical terms. To gear the scientists to the task of writing for farmers is a difficult proposition, mainly because of their bias and preference for research paper writing. To imporve the situation, it is necessary that scientists be given certain incentives and some short term training in writing for farmers. The short term training courses can be organised by agricultural universities and extension departments. This would help them in writing articles in simple language.

A specific reference to the contents of some of the institutional rural publications brought out by agricultural universities, departments of agriculture of the state governments, cooperative societies, etc., would also be relevant. The Govind Ballabh Pant University of Agricultural Science and Technology started publication in 1969 of a rural monthly magazine, *Kisan Bharati*. A content analysis of this magazine for 1985 shows that 76.62 per cent of space was allocated to written material, 7.19 to photographs and line drawings and 15.18 to advertisements. Subjectwise content analysis shows that 81.13 per cent space was devoted to crop based articles, 8.52 to veterinary science articles, 5.54 to home science and 3.77 to agricultural engineering. *Haryana Kheti*, another rural monthly publication, brought out by the Haryana Agricultural University, also devotes itself to crop sciences, veterinary sciences, animal husbandry and home science subjects.

Regarding the ideal content-mix, Jain (1979) has some very interesting observations to make :

> I came to the conclusion in the very beginning that it would not be advisable to harp on agriculture alone, which is a grind. Villagers get sick of it although they have no alternative profession and have to stick around. A paper, in order to catch their attention, has to satisfy their hunger for news – the more spicy the better – of a social as well as political nature. Rural people are relentless gossips. They sit down when they can and gab about this or that matter. This provides them their only entertainment. They are also most well informed about their neighbours.

The rural press, by and large, apart from giving news also gives expression to the concerns of its readers, more than the metropolitan press does, as it is located closer to the homes and hearths of its readers.

One of the most formidable obstacles that a rural newspaper has to overcome is limited sales and circulation which creates a discouraging situation : since the circulation is limited, advertisements will not be readily forthcoming and without advertisements, the paper will find it hard to survive – a dismal situation indeed for any rural paper.

The reasons for the low circulation of a rural newspaper are fairly obvious : urban concentration of newspapers, low rate of literacy, lack of an organised distribution network, absense of a rail head and unsatisfactory transport system in most places, low purchasing power of the rural people and in most cases, prohibitive postal rates, thereby making subscription through the post uneconomical for the papers. In the villages, where newspapers can be delivered only through the postal service, the number of post offices is severely restricted. For instance, in a country like India with 500,000 villages, it is very difficult to have an efficient postal service distribution network. The urban concentration of a newspaper is a common feature in most countries. In India, communication structures are neither rural based nor rural oriented.

An interesting feature, however, is that in spite of the low literacy rate and readership, papers in villages are read out on a large scale. Bhagat and Mathur (1988) have pointed out that low literacy and poor purchasing power are partly responsible for the limited reach of newspapers and magazines in the rural areas. Though circulation of newspapers in India is as low as two copies per one hundred persons, the readership per copy is much higher than in the developed countries. In spite of illiteracy, the press has become a major institution of change in India. Farm women and village elders who are illiterate have newspapers read out to them by other members of the family. It has been pointed out to the growing evidence that even illiterates can be reached through the print media, as generally there is someone in the household who can, and often does, read out aloud to the other family members. It has also been found that there was considerable exposure of the illiterates to the newspapers and magazines through oral readers. A majority of farmers preserve all or some of their copies for future use.

Jain (1979) says : If one were to ask me if there were newspaper readers in the villages, those who want to cull and store information acquired from newspapers, I would say 'Most certainly, yes'. Those among them who can read are our potential readers, those who, without spending their money, want to soak up what they can during their short visit for communicating to their neighbours at imprompt gatherings. Talking of the farmers discussion groups, Jain says that most members can read and news is read out to those who cannot.

Although the practice of listening to the newspaper being read out or borrowing a newspaper from a neighbour, prevalent in India on a very large scale, ensures the dissemination of knowledge and information through the newspaper, it does not help in increasing its circulation.

One of the most effective methods, tried successfully by the author who headed the FICS during 1973-76, in promoting the sales of its farm monthly magazine, *Haryana Kheti*, was through launching a sales and subscription campaign. The method used was simple. All the subscribers on the mailing list of the farm magazine were requested through a circular letter to enrol one more member for the publication. They were requested to pass on the circular letter to their neighbours, friends and the Panchayat Samitis. They were also requested to convey the request by word of mouth. The response was beyond expectations, indeed it was heart warming. Some of the members who had been loyal readers for years wrote back to us after complying with our request. Some others wrote personal letters saying that they had not only conveyed the messages of enrolling more subscribers for the magazine, but also ensured that money orders had actually been sent. Others wrote that they were not getting the magazine regularly.

We were surprised to note that for some of the subscribers, the magazine was the only window to the university which again was the only institution they had known except for the traditional village institutions like panchayat or the village school. The campaign gave us an opportunity not only to increase the sales and subscription of our magazine, but also provided us with excellent feedback from the readers.

During recent years, a large number of organizations dealing with rural interests – agricultural universities, research institutions, agricultural input agencies, cooperative societies and marketing federations – have taken up extension work in the villages. They organise farmers' fairs, field days on demonstration plots, workshops for releasing recommendations on different crops. These occasions provide a valuable opportunity to the publishers of the rural papers and their readers to interact with each other.

Advertising Support for Rural Press

Advertising, which has been confined largely to the urban areas, is now gaining a foothold in rural areas. The reasons are many : massive investment of government funds in the field of rural development resulting in more money in the hands of rural consumers, extension of the electronic media in villages at a rapid pace, and the consistent efforts of commercial enterprises and big business houses to enter the rural market. With planned economic development measures initiated by the government, the village people are emerging as major consumers. Also, the advent of high yielding varieties which has contributed to the economic prosperity and agricultural boom has increased the demand for consumer goods. Several other measures, almost everywhere in the Asian villages – electrification, rural banking, postal and telecommunication facilities and greater interaction with urban areas – are directing the villages towards a market economy. All this, in turn, has led to a boom in rural advertising.

In various fora - be it a seminar on communication problems or rural development, a gathering of media experts or a meeting convened to chalk out a strategy to reach the villages – the role and importance of a vibrant, strong and effective rural press is underlined with great fervour and passion. However, when it comes to advertisement support, surprisingly even the manufacturers and producers of goods and services, who want to reach out to the rural market, show a marked preference for the big dailies which are brought out from metropolitan towns and big urban centres. The editors and publishers of rural newspapers are of the opinion that when it comes to exhorting small and language newspapers to reach out to the rural areas and pay more attention to the issues and concerns of the common people, the government functionaries including ministers are most vociferous; however, the government policies do not measure up to the assurances of assistance to these papers.

The complaint of the small and rural newspapers in the Indian situtation is : whereas in terms of circulation the English language newspapers are far behind the language papers, more than half of the budgetary provision of the central government for advertisement is allocated to the former. More distressing is the fact that advertisements aimed at creating social awareness, directed primarily at the rural masses, are released to the urban newspapers.

In this context, local advertising is the one area which the rural press should sincerely and vigorously strive to capture. With the increasing prosperity and economic activity in rural communities in all countries of Asia, improved transport and communication systems, and accelerated demand for consumer goods, local advertising by the local branches, offices and other commercial advertisements originating from small scale industry will be substantial. Then there are a large number of institutions operating from district headquarters : municipal committees, district courts, banks, etc. They constitute a potential source of advertisements. Additionally, there would be scope for tapping social community advertisements, like notices of births, marriages, obituary notices, political and social meetings, election meetings, etc., in ample measure, which would constitute a rich source of advertisement support.

The participants from various Asian coutries at the seminar on the Development of Rural Press in Asia, organised by the AMIC in November 1986, were of the opinion that potential existed both for readership and advertisement support for the community and rural press in the region. In the above seminar, the Director of Research Institute of Newspaper Development, C. G. K. Reddy, made the following observations which, by and large, sum up the local advertising situation : The need exists for small and rural newspapers, but the rural press must design an appropriate editorial formula that is attractive to the readership in the community. Management must identify the readership and organise itself to reach it. It must also seek the revenue potential and cultivate and exploit the sources fully Just as readership exists which cannot be served by the urban press, so does advertising potential which cannot be satisfied by the bigger newspapers. The small and rural newspapers must convince themselves that a special clientele exists for them and is waiting to be satisfied. The experience of successful provincial newspapers confirms the view that both readership and advertising potential exist, and this can be exploited to their benefit if newspapers prove they can provide something special and distinct from what the big newspapers are able to.

More often than not, most of the rural papers are a single person enterprise – one person working as editor, printer and advertisement manager. He has hardly any training in the fast changing technology of printing. It would not be a matter of surprise if many such persons are unaware of the modern printing technology, offset printing, photo type setting, colour scanners, etc. While a majority of dailies coming out from metropolitan and urban centres in most of the Asian countries have switched over to new technologies of composing and printing, the rural papers are still printed on the old printing equipment. They offer a dull and drab look. Compare most of the rural papers – single colour, hand composed, on inferior quality newsprint – to the urban product, multicolour, computer type set and printed on offset machines. Add to it the better editorial quality, modern methods of circulation and easier access to customers because of better transport network, and one would know why rural papers fare rather badly as compared to the papers produced in urban areas.

The reasons for this sorry state of affairs are not far to seek – lack of skilled technicians, technologists and professionals for different areas of printing and publishing, lack of adequate financial support from banks and other financial institutions, high cost of newsprint, etc. The rural press suffers from these crippling handicaps, impeding the development of a self-sustaining, modern and healthy section of the important field of journalism.

In India, the problem is particularly acute because of the large number of regional languages in which papers are brought out. Since teleprinters in several of the regional languages are not available, correspondents have to send their copy either in English or use some other channel. In the Roman script, there are dozens of fonts available, but in regional languages, the number of fonts available is limited, thus, the use of different type fonts as a display device is the bare minimum. Regional news services as also feature syndicate services, so readily available in English and Hindi, are lacking in regional language journalism. The biggest sufferer would, therefore, be the rural press which has to depend upon these facilities – news services, teleprinter services, feature syndicate services, etc., in English. Translation is a cumbersome and time consuming task. The result is that these newspapers lack an up-to-date, sharp and competitive personality in terms of editorial content, presentable lay out and get up.

No amount of efforts to modernise the rural press will succeed through half-hearted and piecemeal efforts. What is needed is strong financial backing from the government, commercial banks and other financial institutions in providing loans for the purchase of modern printing equipment. The longstanding demand of the small and rural newspapers to classify these printing units as small scale industry, enabling them to receive loans on easy terms, should be conceded, without which modernisation will be an uphill – almost an impossible – task.

Modernisation is a colossal task, particularly in an area like the rural press, which deals with a rather traditional and conservative set up. It cannot be worked out unless there is a concrete, workable and viable policy at the level of both the government and the industry.

High Water Mark of Rural Press

The rural press, notwithstanding numerous bottlenecks and problems, has several success stories and shining examples to its credit which could truly be considered as the high water mark of the rural press.

In China, the Peasants Daily, the biggest national agricultural four page newspaper has a circulation of one million. It began publication as a weekly in 1980 with a circulation of 200,000. Each copy costs about 60 paise, a price most rural families can afford. It sells in all China's provinces including Tibet, as well as ten foreign countries.

It is indeed remarkable to find that, as a rule, every reporter and editor must spend at least two months in the countryside every year during which time they are expected to familiarise themselves with the local peasants, their aspirations and difficulties.

The paper engages 300 peasants as regular stringers and about 700 as irregular correspondents. The paper chooses the most typical letters for publication while referring the rest to relevant organisations. Very often, investigation groups are sent to the countryside if the letters touch upon matters of significance.

In India, apart from rural newspapers and magazines, agriculture reporting in the big dailies from metropolitan cities has done a lot in creating and sustaining interest on rural topics.

In February 1969, the *Hindustan Times* began a feature "Our Village Chhatera", one of the best documented rural feature series brought out in the Indian Press. The purpose was to open a window on rural India for the predominantly urban readership of the newspaper. For years, week after week, a team of enterprising reporters wrote about the village with rare sensitivity and perception. They wrote about the rural scene in depth and in all its versatility. Chhatera had become a household word for thousands of urban readers of the newapaper. No other paper has initiated such a programme of development journalism in spite of the intense interest the feature had created amongst the urban readers about the rural problems.

Several universities, cooperative societies and even individuals have done pioneering work in promoting the rural press. They have used this medium for conveying the message of improved agricultural technology to the farmers, livestock keepers, home makers, etc.

The rural press is potentially one of the most effective media for making a significant contribution to the economic and social development in the vast rural areas of Asia. This medium will, however, have to be developed into an effective channel of communication. Only then will rural newspapers become instrumental in bringing village communities closer and guide and influence decisions at the level of village institutions.

This is important in the context of the vast, varied and heterogeneous Asian society. In Asia, the rural society comprises more than two thirds of the population. That Asia lives in the villages is well known truism. Most of the countries in Asia share the same basic problems and features; limited resources and large populations.

In his fascinating study, Rural Development in Asia – Meeting with Peasants, Gilbert Etienne, gives a detailed and absorbing account of the slow and silent change taking place in the Asian villages. His travels and discussions take him to five countries of Asia – Afghanistan, Bangladesh, China, India and Pakistan – and he concludes that signs of change are apparent in the rural world in Asia : The enormous areas of extreme poverty in east Uttar Pradesh and Bihar are beginning to stir. Jaisalmer in the heart of Thar desert is beginning to emerge from isolation. About China, he says that asphalt or good metal roads are no longer as rare as they were during his first visit to China in 1953. The network has improved. The current rural development strategy of China emphasises liberalisation of the system and the need to diversify the rural economy, creating more employment and income opportunities. Farmers produce more, sell more, which widens the scope for trade, transportation, the manufacture of handicrafts and even, small privately owned workshops.

The doyen of Indian journalists, the late M. Chalapathi Rau, has written, "The future of the Indian press means essentially the future of the Indian language press. India will have gradually mammoth circulation in all the Indian languages." There is no doubt that with increase in literacy and in the purchasing power of the people living in slums in the cities, and in the rural areas, there will be significant increase in the circulation of regional language newspapers, not only in India, but in Asia as a whole.

In a futuristic study on the development of the press in the year 2000, it has been stated that the present public policy against the growth of a monopoly press and in favour of small and medium sized newspapers is likely to continue. The vast size of the country, multiplicity of languages and cultures, and the varying types of regional and local problems also favour the growth of the small and medium sized regional press. With regional development and growth of democratic institutions, a number of newspapers, primarily for the consumption of the literate masses in the rural areas, may also be published. The experience of European countries where the number of newspapers has declined and the concentration of newspapers in the hands of a few groups has increased, is not likely to be manifest in India. Small and medium sized local newspapers will predominate in the country, but despite their predominance, the big papers published from metropolitan and large cities will share a greater proportion of the total newspaper circulation.

It is in recognition of the importance of the rural press that the IPDC has instituted a prize for rural communication, with a view to improving communication in all its forms—more particularly local newspapers, radio and television programmes, printing equipment and films—in rural communities, and primarily in developing countries.

Radio Broadcasting for Rural Development

One of the most disquieting features of the contemporary media scenario in the country is the steady neglect of radio broadcasting. It is because of the unbridled and misplaced enthusiasm, skewed policies and wrong priorities, that in their zeal to promote television during the past decade, radio has been neglected by default.

Wilbur Schramm, in his inimitable manner says, "Television is our glamour girl. When she came to the room, we turned our attention to her, rather than to her plainer sister, radio". This brings us back to the basic question : the priority to be attached to television over radio in allocating national resources.

According to Nikhil Chakravarty (1988); the neglect of AIR is based on a popular misconception that radio in the age of television has no future. This has been disproved by the experience in the West, where television could not dislodge radio as a major means of communication. In America for instance, a 10-year old census showed that the number of radio sets was more than double that of the population : it must be many more now. A radio in the car, kitchen, bedroom and the children's room is a common feature even in lower middle class homes in the USA. Mark Tully, the eminent broadcaster and the former BBC correspondent for Southeast Asia says, "The neglect of radio is all the more extraordinary bearing in mind the fact that millions more Indians have access to radio than to television. Recently in a village near Ghazipur on the Uttar Pradesh - Bihar border I was told that there were only two or three private television sets in the village. When I asked about radio the group villagers as if with one voice, said : oh every one has a radio".

The Working Group on Autonomy for Akashvani and Doordarshan had more than fifteen years earlier recommended that India should give first priority to the development and densification of radio for atleast the next 10-15 years. It had stated : The Working Group is of the view that while television is a powerful and effective medium, there is no doubt that India should give first priority to the development and densification of radio for at least the next 10 to 15 years. Radio is far cheaper and the availability of cheap transistors has made it ubiquitous.

The country, however, has a long way to go before it can even begin to think that it has substantially exploited the potential of radio. Had the recommedation been implemented, the media scenario would have been more vibrant, meaningful and relevant to the needs of the people. At one of the seminars organised by AIR, it was pointed out that while AIR may have lost its primacy in metropolitan and big towns, it is still the main source of news and entertainment in rural areas and the position is likely to continue for many more years for obvious reasons like cost considerations, availability of electricity and high rate of illiteracy. The large number of underprivileged people in rural areas still stick to radio. The cold, discriminatory and poor relations treatment given to the radio during the past 10-15 years only reflects the unrealistic and woolly headed thinking in the government controlled electronic media as well as lack of appreciation for the grass root realities in the country.

India has had a rich tradition of the use of radio for non-formal education programmes, rural development and also for providing various types of learning opportunities and information to the people. The Pune radio rural forum project in India is cited as the most celebrated use of radio in development. Although the project was subsequently discontinued, yet the experience demonstrated that the radio rural forum can be cost-effective in bringing about community development.

A large number of countries including China, Australia, Canada, Italy, Nigeria, Pakistan have reported using radio successfully in reaching "hard-to-reach", rural audiences quickly and quitc inexpensively. Moreover, the relevance of radio as the most effective way of establishing continuous contact with rural population has been well established where extension work is difficult because of the enormous size of the country and lack of roads. Radio is still the cheapest, fastest and the farthest reaching technique for beginning a communication process.

The extensive reach, effectiveness, popularity and acceptability of the radio programmes for rural development are evident from the fact that many of the crop varieties are known in villages at some places as "Radio Varieties", since information on the new strains reached the illiterate cultivators through the radio.

In his study on, *Television for Rural Development*, Rao (1992) points out that as regards reach and utilization of the media and villagers exposure to other informational channels, it was observed that exposure to radio was found to be significantly high, with as many as 80 per cent having access to the medium and getting the benefit of exposure to the broadcasts. Rao also noted that rural/agriculture programmes were high on the priority of listeners. It is encouraging to note that the villagers attach high importance to the listening of rural programmes. The Pune station of All India Radio transmits daily about 60 minutes of farm programmes and has been able to establish itself as an important source of agricultural information. Its Radio Rural Forum programmes received worldwide attention during 1956. It was also observed that as a social tradition women do not go out to public places. Therefore, among those who do not own a set, there is hardly any scope for exposure unless there is a set within the next three four houses.

Local Radio Stations : A Future Vision

In 1983, All India Radio broadcast a series of features under the title India – AD 2000. These programmes tried to project a vision of the future, then 17 years away, from the contemporary perspective and experience. The programmes covered different aspects of life and society and one of the features focused on communication. One of the experts interviewed in the programme expressed the definite view that at the end of the 20th century radio would be the dominant medium in our country (Ghosh, 1988).

As a part of the process of bringing media closer to the heads and hearts of the people and to ensure their greater involvement in the media programmes, the concept of Local Radio Stations has proved most effective.

The local radio stations are ideally suited to the dissemination of farm technology according to agro-climatic regions, farming essentially being a regional industry. The local radio station also ensures programmes in the local idiom and is able to attract greater participation and involvement of the people of the area. The local radio would be their own institution, located in an area and milieu not distant to them. It shall mean to the people, more than a studio far removed from them and located in a far off town. The local station draws talent rooted in the genius of the area and produces programmes suiting their socio-culture environment. It also gives market reports of the business centres where they actually sell their produce, takes note of the weather of the place which is likely to directly affect their crops and inform them of extension programmes at places where they might themselves be participating. The local radio talks which are interesting in language and style are acceptable to the people of the area. In short this local institution invokes strong empathy, in the progress and development of which they have their personal stakes and to that extent their personal involvement.

The local station grows with the people in the soil of the area and does not look like a transplanted and grafted idea. It develops the characteristics of a Village Chaupal – a meeting place for ideas and discussion, a centre for dissemination of information, and has a modernising influence over its audience. While a national hook-up gives news and other centrally produced programmes, it depends upon regional stations for regional news and regional programmes. The programmes, produced at the local stations are mainly in the area of agricultural extension, nutrition, home and family improvement including food storage, fruit and vegetable preservation and rural women, etc. Interaction between regional and local programmes is, of course, essential. Local radio can foster the diversity of cultural traditions, ideas and expressions to further enrich the social fabric of the country.

The Indian experiment in establishing local radio stations began when the AIR ventured into a new phase of broadcasting with the establishment of first local station at Nagercoil in the Kanyakumari District in Tamil Nadu in October 1984.

The comprehensive documentation of the concept, practical utility of local radio for development, expectations and impact of the Local Radio in the Development Communication Report, No. 64, January 1989, provides valuable insight into the working and future prospects of this unique experiment in the cause of development communication.

The establishment of the Local Radio at Nagercoil encouraged the producers to experiment and innovate a new format of broadcasting. Writing about this aspect, Anjaneyulu (1989) says :

> Though small in number, the Nagercoil Local Radio producers geared up to face the challenges posed by the first ever local radio station in a very short period of time. Staff were allowed to waive the audition rules, to deviate from the Fixed Point Chart – a set of regulations and operating procedures – and to engage part time comperes and free lancers for outside broadcasts, reporting, editing and presentation. Nagercoil Radio's success was possible in part because of the latitudes of freedom allowed to the station.
>
> Official guidelines on local radio state that since a local station serves a small area, its aim should be "to reach right into the heart of the community of people" it is expected to serve. A local radio station must be flexible and spontaneous to enable itself to function as the mouthpiece of the local community. It should endeavour to use its microphone to reflect and enrich the life of the society. Its programmes should satisfy the local

aspirations of the people whom the station serves. In short, local radio should identify itself so completely with the interests of its local population that the heart of the people beats in every pulse of the programmes it broadcasts.

This is how Anjaneyulu sums up his impressions about the functioning of the experiment : The first local radio station at Nagercoil has come to stay. Its vitality and vigour have opened up a new future for broadcasting throughout India. The freedom that it offers to express the sentiments, emotions, ideas and views of its listening clientele have the potential to ultimately transform every local station into a People's Radio Station.

During the Seventh Plan period 73 stations were planned to expand the concept of local radio stations, out of which 58 have been commissioned. It is, however, essential to underline that the working of local radio station could be successful only with public participation. Mehra Masani (1976) has rightly observed : Public participation is only possible with local radio. People living in the neighbourhood must take an active part in the day-to-day broadcasts. They must feel that it is their station and not one provided by and run by someone else. Local panchayats, mahila mandals, extension workers, students and teachers, must all be persuaded to work for the station. The absence of professional expertise is made up for by informality, enthusiasm and involvement.

Farm and Home Units

The establishment of Farm and Home Units, in order to provide relevant, timely and local specific information to the farmers of various agro-climatic areas has proved to be very useful programme. The emphasis in these Farm and Home programmes is on a direct method of presentation, dictated by the need to convey hard-core scientific and technical information and quick timely guidance. Due stress is also laid on soil and water management, social forestry, environmental protection and ecological balance in addition to family welfare, nutrition and eradication of social evils.

According to the Annual Report of the Ministry of Information and Broadcasting for the period 1993-94, at present Farm and Home Programmes are broadcast from 92 AIR stations besides all local radio stations. The duration of Farm and Home Programme is 40-60 minutes per day and are broadcast on all days of the week. In the broadcast of rural programmes, AIR can derive great satisfaction at having gradually won the confidence of the traditionally conservative farmers and helping them, through the use of new and improved techniques, to diversify crops, achieve higher production with obvious economic advantage to themselves and the country.

The programme of setting up of Farm School on Air which at present is being broadcast from 15 radio stations has yielded good results. This programme started from Trichur and Vijayawada stations of Akashvani in 1973. According to Luthra (1986), the procedure adopted is to broadcast an intensive training course on some specific agricultural or allied subject. Listeners are registered for each course, examinations are conducted at the end of the course and prizes and certificates awarded to those who are successful. AIR Bangalore's course on paddy cultivation had 23 lessons and Tiruchi's on poultry farming 31 lessons. Nine hundred and fifty farmers registered for Delhi's course on manures and fertilizers. A notable aspect of the scheme is that some of the prizes given to successful farmers are by various public and private organisations, such as state cooperatives (dealing with agricultural inputs like seeds, insecticides, spraying machines and marketing of the produce), fertilizer corporations and nationalized banks.

Public Participation in Rural Programmes

However, what these programmes essentially lack is the participation of the people for whom these are basically meant. These programmes continue to be studio based, comprising mostly talks by experts. The roving microphone concept of the radio programming, where the participants instead of coming to the studio, the radio station is temporarily established in the field and microphones and cassette recorders are taken to the field for recording a live programme needs to be more frequently put into practice. On occasions the programme staff of the radio station visit villages to record the impressions of the people about various welfare and development activities. The people are encouraged to express their views on the manner of implementation of various programmes. Although in terms of cost one such field based programme, as against an ordinary studio based programme, is ten times more costly; and entails far greater effort on the part of the state government officials and the station staff, yet such programmes encourage open debates on issues of public interest and provide the planners and administrators with much needed valuable feed back. Such programmes have greater liveliness and down to earth importance and enable a wider section of listening community to participate.

In the context of serving the small and marginal farmers, Khan (1979) has pertinently pointed out : The programme for small and marginal farmers should aim at educating them in regard to the scientific information which can be relevant to their situation. Small and marginal farmers must be educated in regard to special programmes launched by the Government for their benefit. A case in point is the work done under the SFDA, MFALA, DPAP, dry farming programmes, etc. Such programmes tend to be publicity-oriented. This must be avoided.

The participants from ten Asian countries in a seminar on, Broadcasting in the 80s for Rural Development, organised by the APIBD pointed out that the current practice of radio and television services primarily being used to pass on information to the village listeners from government and government officials had been found wanting. The group recommended replacement of the practice by an approach in which voices of the villagers themselves are heard. This approach would serve a dual purpose – for the edification of the government in its planning for national development and to benefit other villagers in similar circumstances. The participants further expressed the view that the views and experiences of those being in similar conditions and with similar resources can often create a greater impact in spreading useful information than excessive use of "experts."

However, pointing to the inadequacies of the efforts made in the direction, Luthra (1986) says : Over the years most stations and Doordarshan centres have introduced programmes of various types in which queries from listeners about their problems, whether these pertain to law, family size, public and civic services, education, employment are replied to by the experts. There are also programmes in which people participate themselves, or their voices are heard in the form of recordings made by roving teams. However, AIR and Doordarshan themselves would be the first to admit that such broadcasts are still neither adequate nor do these properly cover the whole range of people's problems.

Equally relevant are the observations of H.Y. Sharda Prasad (1981) : I urge once again that as governmental people we should get out of the assumption of the advertising world which believes that the public is gullible. The public on the other hand is very suspicious....(there is) another kind of fallacy of official publicity; namely, the tendency to believe that if you put out more press notes and more satistics you have immediately brought about more conviction. Also that if a Ministry asked the Prime Minister for a message on leprosy more people's minds are changed ..... "We seem to think that coverage is communication, that quantity is credibility."

Television and Rural Development Programmes

Television in India was introduced as an experimental service in September 1959. This experimental service sponsored by UNESCO as a pilot project intended to be educational in nature.

The 1959 memorandum between UNESCO and AIR had described the TV project as "an experiment for assessing the value of different types of educational television programmes suitable for group viewing in rural and urban communities in such a way that the result of such an assessment may be useful not only for India but also other Asian countries in the use of television for community education."

At the time of introduction of television, the official policy stressed that TV was to be used as a medium of social education as well as an instrument to support programmes of social and economic development. Specifically it was stated that TV would be used as a weapon against illiteracy and ignorance, it would bring about awareness among the people of sociological problems and make them conscious of national goals; it would create a sense of participation in India's efforts to usher in a new social order; it would play a vital role in cultivating civic consciousness and respect for law and order, public morality and so forth and, in the field of entertainment, it would mould public taste to higher aesthetic levels.

All these statements of intent to use television for development notwithstanding, while justifying the vast outlay on the expanding TV set-up, even the debate on the use of the medium for development seems to have been lost in the glitter of the showbiz and soap operas. There are, of course, programmes on environmental protection, drug addiction, adult education, consumer protection and agricultural development, but these are relegated to a back slot.

That the Indian television has become primarily a medium for family entertainment and the development programmes do not enjoy large viewership has also been highlighted by a Doordarshan Study. The Study conducted by the Audience Research Unit of Doordarshan during January-March 1993, covering 420 villages from 15 states observed : Though Doordarshan entertainment programmes have large viewership in villages, the development oriented programmes do not have such viewership. Some of the other conclusions of the Study are as under :

1. Regional Programmes

Even regional programmes serve a very large area. The programmes of Bangalore Centre may not be relevant and sometimes not even comprehensible to the people in the northern districts of Karnataka. This lack of local specificity has a bearing on viewership. The developmental programmes of Doordarshan have not been as effective as they should have been because of this factor.

2. Television Ownership

The television ownership though, related to economic prosperity, also appears to be dependent on the availability of regional programmes. In Gujarat, which is one of the prosperous states, there are fewer sets perhaps because there were no regional programmes till recently. The Hindi states of Bihar, M. P. and Rajasthan do not have regional service and the number of sets is also very low. However, in Orissa, the regional service has not been able to motivate purchase of TV sets in the rural areas.

3. Regional Differences

There are wide variations in TV ownership patterns. Punjab and Haryana account for 4 per cent rural population but have 13 per cent rural TV sets. Uttar Pradesh, Madhya Pradesh, Bihar and Rajasthan account for 43 per cent population, but only 33 per cent sets ownership.

4. Viewers Per Set

The total viewership of any programme is not only dependent on the rating but also on number of persons viewing from a set. A common observation is that in villages, each domestic set becomes a community set – attracting people from other households. In this study, information was also collected on the average number of persons watching a particular programme from a particular set. The following are the details about the number of persons watching different programmes from a single set :

Feature film	9	Regional Chitrahaar	10
Chitrahaar	9	Regional serials	6
Serials (Hindi)	4	Regional news	5
News in Hindi	2	Programmes on agriculture	2

Krishi Darshan is the oldest, well established and the best known programme for the rural areas and the farmers. The foresight and the pioneering spirit of the visionary space scientist Vikram Sarabhai and the initiative of M. S. Swaminathan crystalised into this innovative programme. This major television programme has been the subject matter of several studies and surveys. Designed as a pilot rural television project, to telecast agricultural information for farmers in order to improve agricultural productivity, Krishi Darshan programme started on 26 January 1967.

The basic objective of the programme is to familiarise the rural audience with the latest technical and scientific know-how about farming practices, agricultural implements, animal husbandry, rural development programmes; to acquaint the viewers with the importance of health, family planning, personal hygiene, sanitation, etc. as also to provide healthy entertainment.

In order to evaluate the effectiveness of the programme, a survey in the three villages of Hisar district, the hinterland of Haryana, was conducted by two faculty members of the Haryana Agricultural University. The objectives of the study were : to study the TV viewing pattern of rural audience, to ascertain the usefulness of Krishi Darshan programme by the rural community, to identify constraints in viewing the programme, and to undertake content analysis of Krishi Darshan programme.

The results of the study were startling : Krishi Darshan

programme, it was surprising to note even in villages was accorded low priority, and was not watched regularly. The single most important constraint in the way of regular TV viewing was the non-availability of electricity on most days at the time of relay. At times frequent current fluctuation also acted as a detterent. This factor combined with the fact that the relay time of Krishi Darshan did not coincide with the free leisure time of the farmers hampered regular viewing.

Regarding programme presentation, the respondents mentioned that it was not very appealing as most of the programmes were studio based monologues with low visual content and appeal. In their view, interviews with farmers in their fields alongwith their opinions and experiences on various practices would be more useful. The respondents expressed the view that the recommendations of specialists on TV were more related to particular areas of specialisation, whereas they were more interested to learn about "packages" that could be adopted. Moreover, they stated that the majority of the recommendations could be adopted by big rather than small farmers.

> As a large majority of the respondents listened to radio programmes related to farming they felt that they were being apprised about recent practices, more through radio than TV. Radio was noted to be a more credible source of agricultural information even in those households which had a TV set, primarily because the programmes were scheduled at more convenient timings, were regular and most of them were directly concerned with field operations.

The respondents also pointed out that most of the programmes gave the impression that these were mostly studio-based interviews, done with the help of few visuals, mostly charts or written material. Of course, plants, seed samples, seed treatment, method of sowing, etc. were also shown by the scientists who had done their home work. But overall the programmes left a distinct impression that Krishi Darshan was produced, directed and conducted mostly in studios.

The findings of several other studies also confirm that rural programmes on television need to be given sharpness, and thrust so as to make them more useful and relevant to the farming community.

According to the Doordarshan Study, there are many sehemes of providing community TV sets to rural areas – some centrally sponsored, some by state governments and some by local community organisations. During the study, it was found that many villages had community sets. In Tamil Nadu, Haryana and Gujarat, most of the villages and in U. P., Kerala and Andhra Pradesh, more than half the villages had community sets. In other states, fewer villages had such facility. Except in Bihar and A. P., in other states more than half the sets were in working condition at the time of the survey. However, it is essential to make adequate provision for community TV sets at concessional prices to the economically weaker sections, selected groups and institutions working in the area of rural development. Local programming capacity and extensive community viewing will go a long way in bringing the benefits of development programmes to a large number of population.

In order that rural programmes on television effectively serve the objective, it is essential to build a working relationship with extension agencies of the agricultural universities, departments of agriculture and other allied institutions.

Kamath (1972), in his presentation at the Seminar on Software Objectives of Indian Television, held in 1972, which was one of the first such efforts to work out proper television programming, said : If television is considered an excellent reinforcement for extension work, extension will have to fully exploit the potential, and the only way to do so is to consider this activity as a part of the scheduled duty in extension. As long as this is not fully appreciated, television in agriculture is bound to be a failure.

In organising television discussion groups, better results can be obtained with small compact ones, and discussion after viewing could be a good extension activity, when the farmers compare what is said and shown in the programme with their own impressions. Attitudes will then no longer be passive, and the programme will make a more or less direct hit on the members of the groups. Village groups would need considerable assistance, particularly in the initial stages to relate the programmes to their own needs, and analyse the programme to what has been said into "what it is we could do". This is where extension and advisory services can be of excellent use, and carry on from there to the fulfilment of the desires of the group.

Reporting Rural Development : Some Constraints

Reporting rural development has not received the amount of priority and importance in the media that it should have in the Indian subcontinent. This is despite a vast majority of the country's population being based in rural areas where agriculture is the major income generating source, contributing to approximately 50 per cent of national income and investment. This is so despite the fact that massive financial outlays are allocated to rural development programmes. This indeed sounds paradoxical.

Reporting development stories by the media is not as pervasive as reporting politics, conflict or even foreign affairs and defence. It is, by and large, confined to an inside weekly page. And that too by some selected newspapers and magazines. Rural stories rarely get front page treatment or as it is termed the "page one" priority, unless it were a disaster event such as starvation deaths, flood, famine or a policy pronouncement.

One, therefore, naturally asks : Why this apathy towards reporting development subjects? Here it is not necessary to pinpoint some of the obvious and well known facts about media i.e. newspapers generally come out from metropolitan towns and are largely confined to local, or at best, state issues.

According to the popular perceptions, rural development reporting is not considered glamorous, or prestigious enough as political reporting. In the reporter's scale of prestige, rural reporting occupies a very low rung. Every young reporter dreams of becoming a political correspondent and moving around in centres of power rather than take to specialization in rural/agricultural and development reporting. Apart from the elitist bias of the print media and their concentration in urban areas, many journalists are unable to analyse rural issues. The rural sector is so diffused and variegated including agricultural policies and operations, cooperative and development policies, changing village milieu—that it cannot be easily packaged into a neat, well-defined slot. These and other constraints have relegated rural reporting to a back seat in an otherwise blooming and bustling media scenario in India.

However, notwithstanding the above hurdles, there have been some outstanding examples of reporting rural development by noted newspapers in Kerala, specially *Malayala Manorama* and *Mathrubhumi*. These were perhaps the first newspapers in the country to start farm features, allotting one page every week exclusively. In any discussion on reporting rural development, the pioneering role of the Madras-based national newspaper, *The Hindu*, must be underlined. *The Hindu* is one of the few newspapers which had appointed a special correspondent for agriculture. Its column, "For the Farmers Note Book", containing latest research findings and their scope for utilisation in different regions, innovation by the agricultural input industry, etc., was warmly received by farmers. It also stimulated non-farmers' interest in agricultural issues. Economic papers have also begun to give prominence to rural coverage. Likewise, regional press which is coming up very fast with its multi-city editions also deals with the issues of rural and agricultural development in great details. The story of "Our Village Chhatera" narrated by *The Hindustan Times* week after week in the 1960s is too well-documented to bear repetition here. This feature serial blazed a new trail in articulating the concerns and issues affecting the rural life. Activities of agricultural universities, cooperative institutions, public sector corporations handling food, seed, fertilizers, and other rural themes have often found their way to the newspaper columns. All this has made rural development reporting a promising area of journalism, but it is still far from being a part of mainstream journalistic activity. The reason is that development journalism has not as yet emerged as an independent discipline. Since there are generally no openings for agricultural correspondents at senior levels, they have to switch over to general reporting. A case in point is that of the development correspondent of a Chandigarh-based English daily, who had acquired indepth knowledge, background and experience in development reporting but was moved over to general/political reporting.

In China reporting rural development is a highly developed area of journalism. In a paper titled, Rural Development leads to a Press Boom, Wu Yoehui, a journalist from the Xinhua News Agency, Beijing, says that in China rural newspapers are geared to cater to the needs of peasants and rural folk who are showing increasing interest in management techniques and science.

China has approximately 500 newspapers and journals serving peasants. Among these are 25 national and provincial peasant newspapers, usually four-page ones, with a total circulation of 10 million copies per issue, and about 200 perfectual and country papers mostly octavos, with a total circulation of 14.5 million copies per issue. Besides, there are at least 500 rural tabloids each with a circulation ranging from 1,000 to 100,000 copies.

In India, there is no such publication. A well-known development journalist, Bharat Dogra, in his article on Realities of Rural Reporting, has said:

> In the area of technology, it is well known that a significant change has taken place in Indian agriculture during the last two decades or so in terms of the crop varieties that are grown. The area planted by HYVs cereals was less than 100 hectares in 1964-65, now it has increased to over 45 million hectares. The methods used for growing new varieties also differ from the traditional methods and involve the extensive use of expensive chemical inputs.
>
> While this extensive change over has been taking place, has the press really tried to go to the village and find out the impact of this change on a continuing basis? Most of the time what appeared in the press regarding this 'green revolution' was based on exaggerated and distorted official claims. This is not the place to dwell on several distortions and imbalances that this technology choice has caused in India and other countries; suffice it to say that several independent researchers, including those in western countries, have documented these distortions extensively. If only the press had been more alert and documented the impact of this technological change in villages and on the country's economy, it could have played an invaluable role in checking the spread of an undesirable technology. The same can be said of some recent changes in cropping pattern in some areas, for example, paddy in place of maize, soybean in place of the traditional oilseeds and pulses, sugarcane in place of staple food crops, etc.

Again, the press has generally not bothered to investigate properly various development strategies. When a new development strategy to increase production of foodgrains or milk or eggs is announced, majority of journalists appear to accept it innocently without asking searching questions about (apart from the most important one of its likely impact on the poor) the kind of market opportunities this strategy will open up and the commercial interests which will benefit. It is, of course, not necessary to be critical of these, but one must certainly try to find answers to be able to look at the development strategy in a wider perspective.

There may be several reasons why leading newspapers and magazines have, by and large, not succeeded in achieving these various objectives of rural development reporting on a regular basis. This is certainly an important question which the leaders of the profession of journalism in our country should think over.

Where does rural development reporting figure in the list of priorities of electronic media—radio, television and the video? Except for radio, rural development reporting figures very low in the programmes produced by television, while video is totally oblivious of rural development, except perhaps its use in some training programmes.

Radio continues to enjoy greater popularity and acceptability amongst listeners in respect of rural and agricultural development programmes. Excellent programmes produced by AIR's Farm and Home Units have demonstrated the tremendous appeal and scope in reporting rural development issues. Besides, radio continues to be the main source of news and entertainment in rural areas. Therefore, a large number of underprivileged people in rural areas have stuck to radio. Consequently, it is necessary that rural programmes on radio should be strengthened and popularised. Radio is very useful in creating community awareness and action on new devices and processes shedding traditional practices and general outlook of the people in the countryside. Rural reporting on radio should, therefore, keep pàce with the extending needs of the rural people in all areas of their work.

Rural reporting on television should be given new dimension and different meaning. The format, presentation and language of Krishi Darshan programme continue to be highly loaded. Sometimes programmes are highly informative, but often charts make the discussion resemble a classroom situation rather than a dialogue. At times, only the written material is presented. The participation of farmers, so essential for any successful communication programme, is minimum. Overall, these programmes leave much to be desired.

The Working Group on Software for Doordarshan observed : Communication can also help to convert the development programmes into a partnership between the experts and the people, each educating and helping the other. The trouble with many development programmes such as Krishi Darshan is that they are produced within the studio, often with urban men in rural garb. It is mostly an urban view of rural problems or a view of problems of urbanised villages.

Doordarshan will have to go a long way and play an effective role in presenting rural development programmes. It is thus apparent that reporting rural development by the media has taken a back seat. It has found sparse support as an academic discipline. It also lacks sponsorship from the newspaper industry and government. Training programmes for development journalists are almost non-existent. Mid-career courses have not yet made their appearance. The scenario is rather discouraging.

Media Strategies

1. Extension Agency Reinforcement

Radio and TV broadcasting, essentially a part of mass media communication process, share the characteristics and limitations of such a system. In such a system amount of feedback readily available is low, the message flow tends to be one-way and can be used to increase knowledge. Interpersonal medium, on the other hand, tends to be two-way and the amount of feedback readily available is high and is best used in situations calling for attitude formation and change.

Interpersonal medium, which in the context of rural development, would include extension workers in the agriculture and community development departments of the state governments, personnel of agricultural agencies like MAFAL and agro-industries centres and extension set up of agricultural universities and research institutes, would provide necessary reinforcement and supplement media programmes. Coordination between extension agencies and rural broadcasting will make these programmes more purposive and meaningful. These agencies can, in fact, help disseminate information about media programmes including topics and subjects for discussion through numerous magazines, leaflets, folders they bring out regularly and on special occasions like farmers fairs and field days, as a part of their extension activities. They can also involve programme producers and planners in programme formulation and modify programmes to suit the requirement of the target audience.

Such institutionalised working relationship and coordination will help to serve the rural population better and contribute to the tasks of rural development which is the central objective of communication policies and programmes.

2. Rural Channel

An exclusive channel on TV and Radio for rural programmes – Rural Channel – is envisaged for enhancing the quality, frequency and priority of programmes for rural areas. These programmes could also broadcast traditional entertainment and cultural programmes so popular in villages. Development messages, through traditional cultural entertainment programmes are received by rural audience with greater interest. In the absence of such a channel, the felt needs of the rural community get lost or crowded out in the competing demands for entertainment from urban audience.

3. Increased Rural Programmes

More electronic media programmes must emanate from the villages, with common issues and problems and from the farmer's fields. Television must not only produce programmes for the rural people but also of the rural people; let it present what the rural people think of themselves and what solutions do they offer for their problems. Let the television not present, as the Report of the Working Group on Software for Doordarshan, pointed out, "an urban view of rural problems or a view of the problems of urbanised villages."

4. Training Programmes for Rural Journalists

Training programmes for workers in rural development projects like village level workers in communication methods and those of communication practitioners in rural development would go a long way in creating the much needed mutual appreciation of both the aspects. Since, with the expansion of the print media the problems of staff training and recruitment are getting bigger every year, inhouse training should be organised by the newspapers, besides formal training in journalism schools. An appreciation course in rural problems, preferably a rural institute or an agricultural university would go a long way in redressing this deficiency. A Consultancy

Service for the rural press or for those national newspapers who want to report on rural problems, would fulfil the objective in a large measure. It has also been observed that the personnel working in the rural press lack adequate training required to handle their multi-faceted responsibilities. They lack not only adequate editorial ability, but also the perspective necessary to manage various aspects of a newspaper. Rural papers also lack balance – the papers coming out from government or semi-government organisations avoid giving community or political news and thereby fail to create broad interest in the reading public. Training would help the rural journalists not only to acquire the perspective of a complete newspaper, but also to evolve an ideal editorial mix.

5. Bridging the Gap between Policy Formulation and Implementation

There is a greater need for opportunities for interaction between the media men reporting rural development and the policy makers (Planning Commission, union ministries and corporate bodies working in the field of agriculture, rural development, NLM, environment, health and family welfare) so that the yawning gap between policy formulation and its implementation could be bridged to an extent.

6. Journalists Fellowship Awards for Rural Development

It would be advisable to institute Journalists Fellowship Awards for persons working in the area of rural development reporting and communication. The Fellowship would enable the working mediamen, to work during the Fellowship period, on a selected project and make an indepth study of the subject. Salary for the Fellowship period and travel grant would meet the expenses. Such Fellowships have been instituted by the Ministry of Environment, Forests and Wildlife as a part of National Environment Awareness Campaign.

7. Demystifying the Media Profession

Knowledge, understanding and expertise in communication practice and profession should not be the exclusive prerogative of the media professionals. This needs to be extended through a basic training course to all experts and workers, at various levels working in the areas of rural development, health, sanitation and other nation building activities. A basic appreciation of the elements of communication needs to be imparted through appropriate short term courses. Media specialists, sociologists and development planners should work out inter-disciplinary mechanism for identifying the audience requirements, establishing proper feedback systems and extend guidance in the evaluation of effectiveness of communication programmes.

Our Agricultural Future

Delivering the Sardar Patel Memorial Lectures, 1973 on, Our Agricultural Future, Dr. M. S. Swaminathan had said :

> The technology is now becoming available but the mechanism for transferring it to the illiterate and small users in an effective manner does not exist. Ironically, there is a global communication network which makes the latest findings of science available almost immediately to research workers in any corner of the world; but what is urgently needed is such a communication network at the service of the poor farmer in our country. It is not only knowledge that is needed, but an approach which will be able to supply the right knowledge and tools to the right people at the right time and place. The worker on the spot, whether he is an agricultural officer, a teacher, a gram sevak or a social worker, must be able to identify the local problem or need which will act as a catalyst for promoting cooperative endeavour in that area—it may be lift irrigation in one place, dairying in another, pest control in a third, supply of farm machinery or fish fingerlings in a fourth and marketing in a fifth. In this network, the mass communication media, particularly, the radio, television, cinema and the language press, have a very important role to play; so have the research and the extension worker, the education system and the drive for technical literacy.

REFERENCES

Agarwal, Narendra (1977). Agricultural reporting in India – A brief overview. *Media Asia*, 4 (1/2) : 25-27.

AIBD Bulletin (1981). Listen to the People, 6(1) : 5-6, Kuala Lumpur.

Akash Bharati : National Broadcast Trust (1978). Report of the Working Group on Autonomy for Akashvani and Doordarshan, New Delhi; Ministry of Information and Broadcasting.

An Indian Personality for Television (1985). Report of the Working Group on Software for Doordarshan, New Delhi : Ministry of Information and Broadcasting.

Anjaneyulu, K. (1989). Scaling Down : Local Radio in India. *Development Communication Report*, No. 64, pp. 1-2, Washington, D.C. : USAID.

Asian Mass Communication Bulletin (1976). Singapore, *AMIC* 6(3) : 1-4.

Bongartz, Heinz (1993). Development Theories : NGOs and Self Help Organizations. Nepal Foundation for Advanced Studies, Kathmandu, p. 6.

Bordenave, Juan E. Diaz (1979) Communication and rural development, UNESCO.

Bose, Pardip (1988). Violent Society, in *Continuity and Change—Society*. Sesquicentennial Publication, *Times of India*.

Chakravarty, Nikhil (1988). Our priorities need fine tuning. *Times of India*, July 17.

Dogra, Bharat (1984). The Realities of Rural Reporting, *Vidura.*

Dutt, R.C. (1990). Rural Development – Some reflections. *Yojana*, 34(14&15) : pp. 5-8.

Etienne, Gilbert (1985). Rural development in Asia, meetings with peasants. New Delhi : Sage.

FAO (1987). Development Support Communication. Expert Consultation, Rome.

FAO (1987). The paradigm of communication in development : From knowledge transfer to community participation – Lessons from the Grameen Bank, Bangladesh. Development Communication – A Case Study, Rome.

Ghosh, Avik (1988). A Future Vision, in : *Continuity and Change—Society.* Sesquicentennial Publication, *Times of India*.

Gupta, V. S. (1981). Communication Planning – A plea for appropriate communication. *Media Asia*, 8(3) : 156-161.

– (1987). Rural press development in India – Status, factors affecting its growth and future prospects. *Media Asia*, 14(2) : 67-72.

– (1989). Rural Press : Problems and Prospects, New Delhi : Press Institute of India.

– (1989). Case Study of Indian Rural Television : The Krishi Darshan Programme. *Media Asia*, 16(4) : 215-218.

– and Indu Grover (1989). TV and rural folk. *Vidura*, 26 (5) : 13-17.

Jain, G. P. (1979). Rural Press. Seminar No. 235 : 23-25, New Delhi.

Josef, Eschenbach (1977). The role of broadcasting in rural communication – Mass Media Manual. Friedrich Ebert Stiftung-Bonn.

IARI (1980). Agricultural Journalism and Rural Development, in : *Research in Extension Education—Some basic findings*, New Delhi.

Kamath, M. G. (1972). Television and social change – Role of television in agriculture. Paper presented at Seminar on Software Objectives of Indian Television, New Delhi, Feb. 16-19, 1973.

Khan, A. W. (1979). Better information through radio for small farmers. New Delhi. *Communicator*, 14(3) : 47-49.

Kothari, Rajni (1981). Publishing for Rural India, in : *Publishing for Rural Areas in*

Developing Countries. New Delhi : National Book Trust.

Luthra, H. R. (1986). Indian Broadcasting New Delhi, Publications Division, Ministry of Information and Broadcasting, Govt. of India.

Masani, Mehra (1976). *Broadcasting and the people*. New Delhi : National Book Trust.

Ministry of Information and Broadcasting (1993-94). Annual Report. New Delhi : Publications Division, Govt. of India.

Nair, K. S. and S. A. White (1993). *Perspective on development communication*. New Delhi : Sage.

Nair, L. R. (1967). Private Press in National Development : The Indian Example, in Lerner, Daniel and Wilbur Schramm (eds.) *Communication and Change in the Developing Countries*. Honolulu : East West Centre Press.

Prasad, Kamta (1990). People's participation in rural development. *Yojana*, 34(14 & 15) : 15-20.

Rao, B.S.S. (1992). *Television for rural development*. New Delhi : Concept Publishing Company.

Bhagat Rekha and Mathur, P.N. (1989) *Mass Media and Farm Women*, New Delhi, Intellectual Publishing House.

Rogers, Everett M. (1976). Communication and Development – The Passing of the Dominant Paradigm, in : Rogers Everett M. (ed.), *Communication and Development : Critical Perspectives*, Newbury Park, CA : Sage.

Schramm Wiber (1964) *Mass Media and National Development*, Stanford University Press, USA.

Swaminathan, M. S. (1973). Our Agricultural Future-Sardar Patel Memorial Lectures. New Delhi: All India Radio.

Television and its Impact on Rural Areas : A Doordarshan Study in Dua, M. R. and Gupta, V. S. (eds.) *Communication Planning for Socio-Economic Development*, New Delhi : Har Anand Publications.

UNESCO (1986). IPDC News, No. 8.

6

Women Empowerment : Role of Media

VIR BALA AGGARWAL*

Though 1975 was observed as the International Women's Year, 1975-1985 as the International Women's Decade and March 8 is celebrated as the International Women's Day, each year, precious little seems to have been done to uplift the status of women in general. Despite years of world wide struggle and legislations on gender equality, women continue to be discriminated against in every country according to the recently released Human Development Report brought out by the United Nations Development Programme (UNDP). Reports from all over the globe indicate that atrocities on women are on the rise. Though the constitution granted equality of status to women and also gave them the right to vote, in general, women still do not enjoy full equality of status in the society. This is specially true of the vast majority of women in the rural areas, who are illiterate, household and ignorant of their rights under the law.

The successive Five Year Plans have consistently placed special emphasis on providing minimum health facilities integrated with family welfare and nutrition for women and children, acceleration of women's education, their increase in the labour force and welfare services for women in need. Various welfare and development schemes have been introduced to improve the living conditions of women and to increase their access to and control even material and social resources. Special steps have been taken to remove legal,

* Assistant Professor, Department of Journalism and Mass Communication, Himachal Pradesh University, Shimla.

social and other constraints to enable them to make use of the rights and new opportunities becoming available for them. The major thrust of the Sixth Five Year Plan (1980-85) in the field of welfare of women was their economic upliftment through greater opportunities for salaried, self and wage employment. The Plan adopted a multi-disciplinary approach with a three pronged thrust on health, education and employment for women. It was expected that programmes relating to education, health, nutrition and employment would no doubt go a long way in the removal of social disabilities facing women. However, the improvements in the socio-economic status of women would depend to a large extent on the change in a value system, attitudes and social structure prevailing in the country.

The developmental programmes for women continued to grow and more attention was paid to the conditions of women in the Seventh Five Year Plan (1985-90). A significant step in this Plan was to identify/promote the beneficiary oriented programmes for women in different developmental sectors which extended direct benefit to women.

There has been, in general, a lack of awareness among the people about various legislations and programmes being implemented for the benefits of women. Although the socio-cultural situation, to a great extent, keeps women isolated, lately the radio, TV and mass communication media have exposed them to information and knowledge. However, such exposure has not yet resulted in creating consciousness to the desired extent among women, nor has it succeeded in loosening the hold of tradition oriented thinking and mores. The significant role that is rightly women's in such vital areas as attitudes to education, health and health care as well as nutrition and related delivery system, reduction of infant mortality in meaningful participation in many skilled jobs in advanced science and technology areas like medicine and medical research, electronics and informatics, education and teaching, energy conservation and in improving the quality of life, has not yet been grasped fully by society at large.

The Eighth Five Year Plan (1992-97) envisages providing constructive opportunities for expressing the talents and energies of women to enable them to lead the life of dignity and security, and encouraging development through higher participation in all elected bodies and strengthened network of women's organisation. The Plan promises to ensure that benefits of development from different sectors i.e. health, education and employment do not pass women and in view of this, the vigil on monitoring of these sections has been increased. The current Plan also gives greater emphasis on women as equal partners and participants in the developmental process and thereby, the conceptual thinking has shifted from development to 'empowerment of women.'

The decade of women considerably succeeded in generating concern on women's issues both at national and international levels. Besides the emergence of autonomous groups and developmental organisations, gradually realizing the need of women's participation in the developmental activities the decade promoted academic pursuits particularly research on hitherto ignored aspects of women's lives. International conference on Population and Development 1994 held in Cairo, Egypt, also aimed to ensure that all Population and Development policies and endeavours emphasized women's equality. Education, employment opportunities and health services including reproductive health care and family planning are crucial components of women's advancement. ICPD stressed that gender equity issues need to be addressed from a human rights perspective. This requires removing all legal barriers to women's equality, ending violence against women and eliminating administrative, cultural, social and economic obstacles to the realization of women's rights and economic independence.

Change in Women's Status

It is truly said 'the hand that rocks the cradle rules the world'. In the emerging complex social scenario, women all over the world have a pivotal role to play. They can no longer be considered as mere harbingers of peace but are emerging as the source of power and symbol of progress.

In any society the status of women can be viewed in various ways, which are not necessarily mutually exclusive, sex ratio is one of the indicators. The declining rate of females to males in India is exceptional to the general pattern in other parts of the world. The statistics show that it has declined from 972 in 1901 to 929 in 1991. Female infants die at a faster rate than male infants implying social neglect of female health.

Women is the mother of the race and the future of all generations. They are the pivot around which the family moves. They are the source from which various human activities flow and draw inspiration. However, health is one of the important aspects of women's life. National perspective plan for 1988-2000 also recommended (i) health insurance including compensation for accidents for women workers, (ii) preventive health education board, (iii) conversion of piece rate into daily wages to avoid long hours of working to make a meagre living, (iv) providing safety equipment at work places.

Statistics reveal that working women form a substantial proportion of our population. According to the 1991 Census, the total number of working women is 278.35 million, which represents a growth rate of 26.12 per cent. One third of the labour force of India consists of women. During the past decade the percentage increase of working women was double that of male workers. The percentage of women employed in the organised sector has also increased from 11.1 in 1970 to 14.1 in 1991. It is, thus, obvious that female work participation has been increasing over the time. However, in the industrialized countries gender discrimination shows up mainly in employment and wages with women getting less than two thirds of the employment opportunities and about half the earnings of men. The United Nations Development Programme (UNDP) study of available data in 43 countries shows that the female-male wage ratio ranges from a low of 51 per cent in Japan to a high of 90 per cent in Sweden. Similarly, the female male ratio in non-agricultural labour force participation rates varies from 22 per cent in Bahrain to 89 per cent in Finland. The point to note is that it is not 100 per cent in any country. A study conducted by Prof. P. P. Parikh and Prof. S. P. Suhatme of the mechanical engineering department of Indian Institute of Technology, Bombay, indicate that the women engineers in India face discrimination which has forced them to form a separate forum for defending their rights in the male dominated profession. The study says that industries treat women engineers as out-castes and they are given only those jobs for which there are no takers among men. Campus interviews are held only for men and some campaines openly declare ladies not to apply.

With 1990 having been declared as the International Literacy Year, world wide attention is focused on the all important social problem of eradicating illiteracy. A look at the statistics reveals that the female literacy rate has progressively increased from 8.861 in 1951 to 15.341 in 1961 to 21.97 per cent in 1971 to 29.75 per cent in

1981 to 39.42 per cent in 1991. Female literacy rates have been increasing at a faster rate than male literacy rates. The disparity is closing faster. A redeeming picture is that male female disparities in literacy seem to be on the decline in all the states with the increase in per capita income. Haryana has the distinction of bringing about a remarkable reduction of disparities between male and female rates. Despite improving position of female education in India women continue to lag far behind men in literacy in the national as well as state levels in the ratio of 63.68 per cent to 39.42 per cent. Though Kerala has achieved the enviable status of a fully literate state, this achievement has not proportionately benefited the women in the State. It is an established fact that an increase in female education will have good effects on immunization, health, sanitation, bringing up children and family planning, etc.

Role of Media

Welfare of women is a subject of great concern for the society and media has a major role to play in enhancing this aspect. The Committee on Status of Women observed : The content of communication at any given time reflects the pattern of values of the society. The way the subjects dealing with women are treated indicate to a great extent the prevailing attitude of that society towards its women who are half the population are often half the audience. The success or failure of development plans in education, family planning, community development, health and nutrition depends upon the involvement and participation of women. This shows that compared to men, women are underprivileged in many ways and suffer from serious disabilities. Since education is a costly and long term process, it is essential to harness the mass media. However, incidental studies on the impact of mass media indicate that women's exposure to mass media is often marginal and unsatisfactory. It appears that the mass media has not been an effective instrument to inform and prepare women to play their new roles in society. The committee's investigations reveal a general lack of awareness about the rights, problems, opportunities and responsibilities among both men and women. Since government controls a significant section of the mass media, it should set the pace.

A seminar on Doordarshan's role in Women's Equality and

Development by the Centre for Women's Development Studies and the Committee for the Portrayal of Women in the Media made two major points : (i) a very wide distance existed between the national policy objectives vis-a-vis women's equality and development and Doordarshan's present role and programming, and (ii) the general tenor of Doordarshan's programme counter to its stray efforts to be purposive on women's behalf.

Desired Role of Media

A study of women's role in television and radio in five countries – India, Egypt, Nigeria, Canada and Ecuador, proves that women have a long way to go if they are to make any meaningful impact on society through the control of key management and policy making positions.

A major objective for mass media should, therefore, be to do programmes relating to women's status and image since the status of women is directly related to a country's national development.

Clear guidelines on positive portrayal of women should be evolved. Policy makers should be sensitized to issues relating to women.

There should be systematic crusade against atrocities on women through meaningful programmes.

Media should encourage women to participate in politics. They should be given a special role in our planning process. They should be brought into the main stream of national development not as beneficiaries but as contributors and partakers alongwith men.

Attempts should be made to integrate the message of equality with general programmes aimed at mixed audience to disabuse their minds of prejudice and false concepts.

Thus, there is an imperative need to develop an integrated multipronged strategy to handle the problems of women in all their dimensions. Given strong measures, cooperation and commitment of the general masses and vigorous implementation of the schemes without delay, there is no reason why the women of India should continue in the role of inferior, oppressed and exploited beings, completely dominated and over-awed by men.

REFERENCES

A Project to Mobilise Women (1994). *The Hindu*, July 10.

Census of India (1991). Report.

Eighth Five Year Plan (1992-97), New Delhi : Planning Commission, Government of India.

India Urges Larger Role for Women (1994). *The Times of India*, June 3.

International Conference on Population and Development (ICPD), Cairo, Egypt, September 1994.

National Perspective Plans for Women (1988-2000), New Delhi.

Op. Lit. (1991). Census of India.

Op. Lit. (1991). Census of India, Report.

Prasad Nandini (1994). *A vision unveiled, Women on Television*, New Delhi : Har Anand Publication.

Seminar Report on Doordarshan's Role in Women's Equality and Development.

Seventh Five Year Plan (1985-90). New Delhi : Planning Commission, Government of India.

Sinha, Anjana Maitra, (1993). *Women in a Changing Society*, New Delhi : Ashish Publishing House.

Sinha, Arbind K. (1987). *Mass Media and Rural Development : A study of village communication in Bihar*, New Delhi.

Sixth Five Year Plan (1980-85). New Delhi : Planning Commission, Government of India.

Towards Equality (1975). A Report of the Committee on the Status of Women. As quoted, in *An Indian Personality for Television*, vol. I., p.138.

Women Engineers Face Discrimination Study (1994). *The Times of India*, June 6.

Women Still at Receiving End (1994). *The Times of India*, 4 June.

Women Still at Receiving End (1994). *Ibid.*

7

National Unity and Media Practice

Nationalism, all through the history of mankind, has been one of the most powerful urges that moves a people, and it is around this feeling of nationalism that cluster sentiments and traditions and a sense of common living and a sense of common purpose.

Nationalism, inspite of the recent events in several parts of the world, involving ethnic and ideological conflicts is still universal in its influence and appeal. The nationalist ideal, by and large, in most of the countries is deep and strong. The abiding appeal of nationalism to the spirit of man has to be recognized and respected. Nationalism is not the product of one age, nation, class, party, religion or philosophy, but that each has partly contributed to its growth, partly counteracted it, though in very different degrees.

National consciousness is a pre-requisite and a determinating factor for national unity. National unity, to a very large extent, would depend upon one's perception and concept of nation.

The word *nation* conveys fascinating nuances and connotations. It conveys to the German mind the impression of a great powerful and highly civilized people with its own State, and national is employed only for such lofty concepts as national honour, national unity, the national flag. In Burke's view *nation* is not merely a multitude of human beings living together, but a historical personality with a specific political and social structure, united by a sort of tacit consent and guided by a small class trained in politics and public service and embodying the national traditions. Frederick Hertz, in his seminal study *Nationality in History and Politics* (1966), points out to the wide spread modern usage of nation which identifies a nation with a people constituted as a state. In his view every state forms a nation and every citizen is a member of the nation. This definition, of course, is an exclusively legal one. Many states were or are composed of different nationalities. The Scots, the Welsh and the Irish regard themselves as nations, though they live in a common state with the English. Therefore, in modern history, the moving force is not the legal concept of nationality but the social and emotional force of national consciousness.

The word *nation* is used in different senses and its meaning has changed during the course of time. Different nations, and even different parties within a nation often have different connotations according to the interests they pursue.

Several tendencies and attitudes have been attributed to nation and nationalism and different elements – cultural, linguistic or even religious – have been emphasised by different parties on different occasions and in different contexts. It is however accepted that, by and large, nationalism represents ardent love of the people, unrelenting fight for its true interests, protection against foreign interference and aggression, safeguarding its traditions and stressing of national unity and solidarity; and of course subordination of particular interests to those of the nation.

A nation, like the tribal, local and professional groups, is a self-conscious group, but unlike the other groups it comprises millions of people belonging to a variety of sub cultures speaking different languages and professing different religions, all of whom feel they are one. Nationalism thus involves the will of the people and leads to the formation of a national government. It also implies that interests of the nation are more important than interests of any individual or groups within it.

However, cohesive these groups within a nation may be, these could not be entirely homogeneous. They are bound to be diverse in terms of language, religion, economic and literacy status, etc. Forces of nationalism, in order to succeed the onslaught of divisive forces, have to assert themselves through different media, implementing the national policies and counteracting the forces of disintegration and disunity.

Nationalism or national consciousness is complex and abstract. As Hans Kohn has written, nationalism is a set of mind. It is the result of social learning. This feeling of national consciousness could be generated only over a period of time, overcoming a large number of obstacles and barriers, vested interests and countervailing influences.

Having attempted to lay down the broad definition of nationalism, how do we go about forging national unity? Should as important an issue as that of national unity, which encompasses the whole nation, cutting across communities, languages, regions and religions be left to the government policies; or should it be left to the political opinion leaders of the country to espouse the cause of national unity, or would media alone be able to cope with this challenging task which has more to do with the thoughts, aspirations and attitudes of the people than with attainment of merely quantifiable targets designed to fulfil a laid down schedule.

> National unity, by definition, is a national objective. It cannot be viewed as just an elitist affair. It cannot be confined to particular groups or classes of people – whether social, religious, economic, political or intellectual. Its objective has necessarily to be a super person or national character which transcends and binds together people of every type, profession, region, creed, caste or race in the country into a single identifiable whole.

Role of Media in Forging National Unity

Having stated that the task, which cannot be left either to the political leadership, elite groups or the intelligentsia alone; what role can the mass media possibly play in this crucial task.

In his book, *Nationalism and Social Communication*, Karl Deutsch points out that presence of ample communication facilities is the single most important feature that makes for the development of nationalism. Deutsch goes to the extent of proposing functional definition of nationality 'which consists in the ability to communicate more effectively and over a wider range of subjects with members of one large group than with outsiders'. Easy accessibility to means of communication facilitates social contacts, travel, knowledge of history and culture. Communications help develop a broad and catholic outlook as opposed to insular and local. Deutsch calls such people as, *mobilised population of the country*, who are mobilised by intensive communication with others, directly and indirectly. The frequency and intensity of communication with and within different parts of a country would certainly go a long way in encouraging the forces of national unity at people-to-people level. Likewise communication is seen, *as a kind of temperature controlling agent*. Through the stimulation of aspirations, "Social temperature" can be raised, and the other way round, by providing explanation, the temperature can be lowered.

Two of the main functions of communication, listed in the Report of International Commission for the study of communication problems, 'Many Voices, One World', are :

> *Integration :* The provision to all persons, groups and nations of access to the variety of messages which they need in order to know and understand each other and to appreciate other's living conditions, view points and aspirations.
>
> *Socialization :* The provision of a common fund of knowledge which enables people to operate as effective members of the society in which they live and which fosters social cohesion and awareness thereby permitting active involvement in public life.

These two functions, alongwith others like Debate and discussion and Motivation, underline the critical role that the communication media can play in fostering national unity.

Touching Faith in the Efficacy of Media

It is again intensely interesting to note as to how some of the developing countries have almost touching faith in the efficacy of media as an instrument for forging national unity. In Nigeria media is viewed as a *national unifier.* In the Nigerian context the mass communicators are expected to :

> Perform the unique role of aggregating and articulating the interests of the people, giving them leadership, enlightening them and pleading their cause with the government in a plural society.
>
> Gather information about the problems, needs and interests of the people, and communicate them to the appropriate decision making centres. Besides mass media in a pluralistic society should see itself as the melting pot where various cultures dissolve and merge into one national culture.

In China, mass media alongwith face-to-face communication was effectively used for national integration. The media in China focused popular attention on developing China industrially into a modern state. The media have portrayed regional developments in the context of national progress and unity. Just as television enabled Americans across the country to laugh at the same jokes, the media in China has greatly increased the number of terms, news items, stories and personalities that the Chinese people now can share. The end result is a *much enhanced national awareness*. This enhanced national awareness has mobilized the Chinese people in a way that they are now more ready psychologically to be integrated into the new institutions.

These general conclusions form a part of the Michigan studies on China, Communications and National Integration in Communist China, as the title of the publication. The study, which is a fascinating account of the use of mass media by the Chinese communist party for its political and ideological use, points out that the media cannot create national integration by themselves. The study also underlined the role of radio and films being oral media, as being more adapted to rural audiences, whereas newspapers, journals and books being more suited to urban and educated residents. However, the study affirms that the *media cannot create national integration by themselves.*

In his book, *The Third Wave*, Alvin Toffler (1975) points out that as Second Wave societies began to build national economies, a basic shift in public consciousness became evident. The Second Wave swiftly multiplied the number of people with a stake in the larger world. Bit by bit, psychological horizons expanded. The new mass media increased the amount of information and imagery from far away. Under the impact of these changes *localism faded*. National consciousness stirred. Since the author of Future Shock and the Third Wave credits mass media with stirring the national consciousness, the practitioners and scholars of mass media have lot to feel cheerful about.

Media Policies

In India the primary objective of the national policy regarding the use of mass media is to strengthen national unity. Some of the important guidelines and principles are :

1. Among the nine objectives laid down for Doordarshan, the

first two are : to act as catalyst for social change and to promote national integration.

2. Likewise, the principles guiding newspolicy for broadcast media issued by the Government of India interalia state :

The style and methods of newsreporting should reinforce the fundamental principles on which national policies are based. These fundamental principles include territorial integrity, national integration, secularism, maintenance of public order and upholding the dignity and prestige of Parliament, state legislatures and the judiciary.

3. The statement of objectives, or the charter for the National Broadcast Trust, as envisaged in the Akash Bharati Report, recommended interalia, that the Trust shall :

(i) Uphold the unity of the country and the democratic values enshrined in the Constitution,
(ii) Safeguard the citizens right to be informed freely, truthfully and objectively on all matters of public interest, national or international,
(iii) Provide a national broadcasting service, predominantly Indian in content and character,
(iv) Produce and transmit varied programmes designed to awaken, inform, enlighten, educate, entertain and enrich all sections of the people with due regard to the fact that the national broadcast audience *consists of a whole series of publics*, and
(v) Uphold the secular ideal and promote a spirit of truth and enquiry in the country and among all sections of the people.

The Working Group also underlined the imperative need to propagate a *national approach* to India's problems, and to develop a national consensus on issues which concern the country as a whole.

4. The Press Council of India, likewise, while keeping in view that India is a country with a vastly diverse and differing range of languages, communities, regions and also with varying degree of economic prosperity suggested that the Press, in order to achieve national unity, should emphasise those aspects of the national life which underline the common features of diverse faiths and religions and subordination of sectional interests to national unity and integrity. The Council was, however, emphatic that the writings,

which merely set forth or explain the grievances of a community, be it in any field social, political or economic and are meant to ventilate the grievances of a particular linguistic group or regions should not be considered communal. The Press Council laid down the following guidelines as offending against journalistic proprieties and ethics :

1. Distortion or exaggeration of facts or incidents in relation to communal matters or giving currency to univerified rumours, suspicions or inferences as if they were facts and base their comments on them.
2. Employment of intemperate or unrestrained language in the presentation of news or views, even as a piece of literary flourish or for the purpose of rhetoric or emphasis.
3. Encouraging or condoning violence even in the face of provocation as a means of obtaining redress of grievances whether the same be genuine or not.
4. While it is the legitimate function of the Press to draw attention to the genuine and legitimate grievances of any community with a view to having the same redressed by all peaceful, legal and legitimate means, it is improper and a breach of journalistic ethics to invent grievances, or to exaggerate real grievances, as these tend to promote communal ill-feeling and accentuate discord.
5. Scurrilous and untrue attacks on communities, or individuals, particularly when this is accompanied by charges, attributed misconduct to them, as due to their or of a particular community or caste.
6. Falsely giving a communal colour to incidents which might occur in which members of different communities happen to be involved.
7. Emphasising matters that are apt to produce communal hatred or ill-will, or fostering feelings of distrust between communities.
8. Publishing alarming news which are in substance untrue or make provocative comments on such news or even otherwise calculated to embitter relations between different communities or regional or linguistic groups.
9. Exaggerating actual happenings to achieve sensationalism and publication of news which adversely affect communal harmony with banner headlines or in distinctive types.

10. Making disrespectful, derogatory or insulting remarks on or reference to the different religions or faiths or their founders.

All these statements of objectives, policies and guidelines however do not always translate themselves into ideal writings and programmes furthering the objectives of national unity.

The task of media in fostering national unity is made difficult by bureaucratic thinking, countervailing powerful caste and communal interests and political ideology. The government control and policies framework has an inhibiting and restrictive influence on the quality and nature of programmes put up by the electronic media in the country.

One of the important programmes on Doordarshan – the National Programme – broadcast simultaneously from all the TV centres at the Prime Time from 8.30 to 10.30 p.m. cannot claim to attract the national viewership throughout the country. The programme has not been received favourably by several states particularly in the South, some of whom have discontinued the Hindi news. The programme was also considered an imposition of Hindi on non Hindi stations. Since most of the programmes are from Delhi, contributions from other parts of the country are not represented. An other serious objection was that this compulsory relay from Delhi took away the prime time from the stations' own regional programmes. Such efforts at centralised programme presentation only go on the show that a country of India's size and diversity cannot fruitfully have a single set pattern for its media content.

It is inconcievable that Doordarshan should have ignored the strong feelings that its programmes in Hindi have aroused in other parts of the country.

> "The main thrust of Doordarshan is not only the conversion of the South to Hindi and the northern way of life but to obliterate by indirect means the culture of the South.
> It is a kind of psychological warfare that has been unleashed on the South. All the resources of Government of India are employed by Doordarshan to impose not only Hindi but the superior Northern Culture", R. Gopale Krishana*.

* *The Illustrated Weekly of India*, December 21-27, 1986.

Cultural alienation of people, linguistic differences or communal conflicts can be a threat to the unity of a country anywhere in the world. At one time Canada's internal crisis over Quebec and heightened bitterness between French speaking and English speaking Canadians had created the real possibility of national disintegration. The French Prime Minister Pierre Trudeau, fighting to preserve the national unity had warned, "if certain centrifugal tendencies fulfil themselves, we will have permitted this country either to break up or to become so divided that its existence and its ability to act as one nation will have been destroyed."

Unidimensional View

There have also been murmurs of protest over the Delhi centric view of India, projecting the problems of Delhi as national problems and the Delhi perspective of issues as national perspective. Even the most insignificant occurrence in Delhi becomes a national event, with extended TV coverage, whereas important events in other parts of the country are either not taken note of, or if noted, recede into a background slot. The result is : while Delhi mostly sees itself, the rest of India sees mainly Delhi and occasionally glimpses of India as seen by Delhi.

Surely, this unidimensional view of India is not an inevitable result of space technology. This single view, beamed to TV audiences every day may succeed in bringing about unity through homogenisation, but is it this kind of unity we desire? What happens to the ideal of unity in diversity? (Chitnis, Karnik, 1983).

In a scathing indictment of the Delhi-centric view of Doordarshan, Sevanti Ninan says : When you step very far back from Delhi – say as far back as Kerala – and look at Doordarshan's national concerns from there, it does seem that both government and private TV produces in the capital are suffering from the delusion that this Punjabi – Haryanavi capital is India. Seldom can they bring themselves to look beyond it.*

National Image

What is the national identity or the national image that Doordarshan

* *The Hindu*, 3 July 1994.

generally projects : that of the 200 million middle class as against 350 million subsistence level population, or that of the urban milieu as against the village culture which is still the prime factor in the Indian economy and the politics; or the Hindu and the Hindi culture – a mix of religious and linguistic pot pouri; the dominant culture, yes, but by no means the single or even the most representative of the trends. The rich diversity of the cultural and linguistic fabric of the country – Dravidian, Tamil, Bengali, North-Eastern, are represented in the National Programmes rarely; more as an exception than as a rule. No wonder TV programmes as telecast in the National Channel have certain artificiality about them.

Articulating the above perspective, Anand Mitra, in his seminal contribution, Television and Popular culture in India, points out :

The issue of the Indian image provides the opportunity to re-examine the notion of the nation. Working out of a historical perspective and then considering the internal contradictions in a nation, it is possible to rethink the nation as the articulation of a variety of contradictory practices, where the practices of a dominant social block are represented as the national practices. Around these practices of a Hindu-Hindi hegemony, a national identity and a nation is imagined. Doordarshan as a state controlled medium, is able to represent these practices as the national practices. Doordarshan is able to articulate itself with the national practices thus reproducing and circulating a limited set of practices as the preferred practices of the Indian nation. These are the practices that reproduce the image of India as *bharat*, where the rule of *dharma*, as embodied in the Mahabharat and Ramayan, as reproduced as natural, unequivocal and preferred. This is articulated with the emerging Hindu reawakening, where the notion of a non-secular Hindu state is increasingly becoming predominant.

India, at present, is also riven with numerous conflicting and fissiparious tendencies which threaten the very basis of national unity.

In such a situation how could the media meet challenges facing the country. Certainly not through laying down guidelines or issuing directions alone.

The media will have to come up with certain unconventional, innovative, path breaking and courageous steps. It will have to greatly modify the tendency of projecting only the point of view of the government, the administrators, planners and the policy makers.

The voices of dissent, anti establishment and opposition, however unpalatable it might appear to the powers that be, should be given an equal opportunity to be articulated. An environment of openness, an easy accessibility to the divergent views, a tolerant attitude towards opposing ideologies will help bring down temperatures all around.

In a free society media cannot be expected not to report what it percieves to be truth as it sees it. At the same time it may not contribute to inflaming passions on sensitive issues. I remember how a particular issue of a video magazine, through its on-the-spot filming of the scene of self immolation of a young student during the tension filled days on reservation issue in July 1990 had suddenly aroused passions throughout North India and encouraged several young boys and girls to take their lives for what they considered to be a worthwhile cause. The point at issue is : should not video reporting/filming have been suitably edited so as not to have given rise to separatist, divisive and palpably harmful tendencies in the society?

The disadvantaged and depressed sections of the society feel that their living conditions, their aspirations and even their success stories do not make news unless something out of the way, violent or even bizarre happens to them. In the William Allen White Centennial Seminar in 1969, Carl Rowen had pointed out that the grievances of negroes hardly receive any coverage in the American media unless something volatile happens. He stated :

The truth today is that someone who legitimately speaks for thousands of negroes, who articulates their hopes and frustrations, can show up in most American cities and get no better than routine press coverage. But let a negro show up who says: "If you don't do this or that we're going to burn down this damned town." I guarantee you he'll make front page headlines and all the TV shows.

How prophetic his observations are, when viewed in terms of contemporary scenario in the United States. The media must therefore concern itself with the grievances, problems and issues impinging upon the depressed and deprived section of the society on the continuing basis, and not only when the lid blows off.

It is apparent that once a programme is targeted and slotted as a National Unity programme, it is considered merely as so much of propaganda. The well known cinema producer Khawja Ahmed Abbas points out that making films on national unity is a risky business which few are prepared to take up. He had made three films—*Hamara Ghar, Saat Hindustani* and *Do Boond Pani*, and the last two got National Award as the year's Best Feature Films on National Integration theme; but box office wise all the three were flops. What is therefore needed is a more subtle approach with no direct preaching of the moral, which is always counterproductive. And that is what most of our programmes on national integration on Doordarshan turn out to be.

It must be conceded that while mass media do play a vital role in fostering national unity, it is powerless against mighty forces of casteism, religion and fundamentalism. Media must not be exalted as the 'begetter of all beneficient change or guardian of all that should be cherished. Despite the considerable influence of media, it would be wrong to attribute to it more virtues, more faults or greater powers than it truly possesses. At the same time it is incumbent upon the media practioners to also consider whether truth, if it is going to offend, inflame passions or cause fissures in the society and the country, should it not be better unsaid? I myself find it very difficult to accept the above axiom. But should not we ask ourselves; even if a particular event is true, does it at the same time promote goodwill and does it serve the larger interest of the society? If that happens we would have done our duty by the society, nation, apart from our profession.

REFERENCES

Agee, Warren K. (1969). *Mass Media in a Free Society.* New Delhi : Oxford and IBH Publishing Co.

Akash Bharati – National Broadcast Trust (1978). Report of the Working Group on Autonomy for Akashvani and Doordarshan. New Delhi : Ministry of Information and Broadcasting.

Chitnis, E. V. and K. S. Karnik (1983), Technological options help us get what we seek. *Communicator*, XVIII (3-4) : 24-28.

Eapen, K .E. (ed.) (1989) Role of Radio in Growth and Development. Bangalore : Mass Media Education, Research and Information Centre.

Gandhi Darshan Samiti (1982). National Integration and Communal Harmony, New Delhi.

Hertz, Frederick (1966). *Nationality in History and Politics.* London : Routledge and Kaugan Paul Ltd.

Kunczik, Michael (1984). Communication and Social Change. Friedrich-Ebert-Stiftung, Bonn.

Kuppuswamy, B. (1976). *Communication and Social Development in India.* New Delhi : Sterling Publishers Pvt. Ltd.

Liu, Alan P. L. (1971). *Communications and National Integration in Communist China.* The Centre for Chinese Studies, University of Michigan. Bombay : Oxford University Press.

Luthra, H. R. (1986). Indian Broadcasting. New Delhi : Publications Division.

MacFarlane, Andrew (ed.) (1987-88), *CAEJAC Journal.* The Commonwealth Association for Education in Journalism and Communication, University of Western Ontario, London, Canada.

Mitra, Anand (1993). *Television and Popular Culture in India*. New Delhi : Sage.

Ninan, Sevanti (1994). Capital conceit. Media Pulse. *The Hindu*, 3 July.

Toffer, Alvin (1975). *Future Shock*. London : Pan Books.

8

Environmental Protection and Media

In a leading article – Man, the victim losing hope, *The Tribune*, in its Sunday edition of 19 November 1989, brought out the world view of Indira Gandhi. The article was essentially her memorable speech delivered at the United Nations Conference on Human Environment at Stockholm on 14 June 1972.

This noteworthy effort was important for more than one reason : Stockholm Conference marked the beginnings of environmental revolution; the address itself was remarkable because it went beyond the immediate problems of environmental degradation, pollution, industrial waste, etc. and tried to establish man's link with nature; but more than that, it signified media's commitment to the cause of environmental awareness and sustainable development.

The catalytic and stimulating role of media in creating awareness, in reporting the activities of action groups, grass root movements and voluntary agencies; in informing the readers of the trends and perspectives at the global level and above all, in performing the watch dog function, has been widely recognised.

One of the first issues projected in the media way back in early seventies was threat to the world famous historical monument – the Taj Mahal – as a result of location of a petroleum refinery at Mathura – at a distance of barely 40 k.m. from Agra. Immediately after the foundation stone of the refinery was laid by the Prime Minister, Mrs. Indira Gandhi in October 1973, muted protests by several public spirited persons were beginning to be heard. Protest letters were written to the newspapers, questions were raised in the Indian Parliament and public opinion was sought to be created about the safety of the Taj and other historical monuments at Agra. Several societies, learned bodies and institutions including the prestigious

Indian Heritage Society, the Bombay Natural History Society and the Archaeological Society of India, were involved in the mounting campaign launched to save the precious world famous monument and the nearby Bharatpur Bird Sanctuary. The awareness created due to sustained efforts through the press and series of articles and editorials that appeared in leading newspapers made the government sit up and appoint an expert committee to examine the dangers to the Taj. These sustained efforts, through the press, resulted in the government agreeing to closing down the two thermal power stations located at Agra and shifting the existing small scale industries and foundries to an area beyond the Taj, apart from provision for establishing a green belt between Agra and Mathura. An other welcome decision with long term implications was to create facilities and expertise for building up environmental research within the country.

The media played a notable part in carrying forward the message inherent in the *Chipko* movement, which basically is the movement for protecting environment. Today *Chipko* has become an important word in the laxicon of environmentalists the world over. The *Chipko* movement, received sustained media attention in the country, is probably the world's most well known grass roots eco-development movement. *Chipko* activities have attracted the attention of environmentalists, Gandhians, various people interested in the process of social change and the media personnel throughout the world.

The non-violent, action oriented *Chipko* movement has greatly helped unite the people and focus attention on the mismanagement of forest resources. It's Gandhian character has brought it considerable sympathy. One line of thought is that the main objective of forest management should be soil and water conservation : forests do not bear timber, resin and foreign exchange but soil, water and pure air. The self-sufficiency of the hill people in food, clothing and shelter is important but is secondary to the major ecological objectives. This cannot be achieved unless all commercial green felling is stopped and no new contracts entered into with industrialists to supply raw material. Another philosophy behind the *Chipko* movement is the belief that no conservation is possible without the cooperation of the people. Eco-development strategies will inspire the poor when they are based not just on ecology but also on the needs of the people.

The media has also drawn attention to danger to life from foul environmental conditions, as in the Chembur belt of Bombay : or the degradation of living conditions because of foul water and air, as a result of industry effluents dumped irresponsibly everywhere. Several newspapers and magazines have regular columns on subjects like Environment, Ecology, Wild Life, Conservation and Pollution.

An interesting feature of the environmental reporting scenario in the country is the public interest litigation launched by social activists to protect green belt in towns from enchroachment at the hands of municipal corporations and builders. The fact of the matter is that the courts of the country have come to the rescue of environmentalists where the local administration or the government failed to take effective measures to enforce legal provisions. Reporting of such cases has led to more active interest in protecting the environment. Likewise the ineffective working of the Boards for Prevention and Control of Water Pollution, lack of political will to enforce anti-pollution laws, loop-holes in the anti-pollution legislation have helped create a body of public opinion alert to meet the situation.

The Indian press has also succeeded in highlighting the ill effects of big dams, which resulted in Government's decision to abandon the Bodhghat project on the Indravati river in Madhya Pradesh, pending a fresh reappraisal of its impact on the environment. The media also focused its attention on various 'environmentally destructive developmental projects'. The three month old campaign – Save the Western Ghats march – during 1987-88, a unique 3000, k.m. *padyatra*, Walkathon, covering Gujarat, Maharashtra, Goa, Karnataka, Kerala and Tamil Nadu involved more than 200 non-governmental organisations.

The press has also been performing a watch dog function in monitoring the progress of several high budget ambitious plans launched by the Government of India. It has come out with several incisive reports on the progress made by several projects estimated to cost more than US $ 400 million during the Seventh Plan period. Similarly, other projects on reclamation of wastelands and afforestation are being frequently documented for public scrutiny.

The Hindi language and regional press has been highlighting environmental issues more often and with deeper perception, as it has closer grass root contacts with people directly affected by environmental degradation. The Hindi national daily *Jan Satta* from the Indian Express group, has a weekly column devoted exclusively to development and environment. It has come out with several articles on air pollution in New Delhi and pollution caused by stone crushing industry and thermal plants in areas in immediate vicinity of the capital. Some other issues which the regional press has highlighted are : the polluted lakes, fuel shortage hardship caused as a result of disappearing forests, etc. Earlier the Kerala newspaper *Mathru Bhoomi* has supported the campaign to preserve Silent Valley free as a 'gene pool' to study. Even outside Kerala, Mathru bhoomi's Delhi correspondent organised support in the national capital. The *Hindu*, which pays special attention to science and technology also committed itself to the cause. The district press reflects the concern that the common people feel at the deterioration in soil condition and fertility of land due to industries springing up on areas close to urban settlements.

The programmes telecast on Doordarshan are basic and educational in nature. The two well known documentaries – David Attenborough's Our Living Planet : and Survival provided rich information on nature, wild life and eco-system as a whole. One of the serials in Hindi *Rakshak*, sponsored by a leading Indian business house, pointed out graphically and in detail the threat posed to the beautiful Dal lake in Srinagar, because of construction of hotels and discharge of affluents and pollutants from house boats and dumping of mud and city wastes.

However, these TV programmes, mostly on ecology, deforestation and conservation in rural areas should have been dubbed in Hindi and major regional languages, so that they could have been telecast in regional slots from local centres. It is inexplicable as to how do we serve the purpose of promoting environmental awareness, if such programmes are confined only to English knowing audience, who are in any case, better informed, due to their educational background and broader exposure to mass media, than the rural folk. And programmes on deforestation failed to point out the responsibility of the state governments in the area of afforestation, where there has been more of lip sympathy than real concrete action.

Environmental Reporting : Constraints and Complexities

Environmental reporting is not without its complexities. Environment still does not make news and headlines, unless the story has political ramifications. Environmental news, even now for most of the times, consists of research studies and reports of seminars from international bodies like UNEP, WHO, ESCAP. It is as yet, an evolving discipline, if it could be so termed with much too large a canvas to look after. Since environmental issues cover subjects including air pollution, deforestation, desertification, ecosystems, pesticide pollution, toxic chemical and metals, it is naturally difficult to do justice to a particular subject without adequate background material and a certain basic appreciation of the subject. And this is indeed a tall order for a "generalist reporter".

The ESCAP in its publication : Reporting on the Environment, has defined Environmental Reporting as :

> To define environmental reporting just by the issues it includes may be too narrow. A much broader definition states that, since the environment involves the active relationship between people and their living and non-living environs, there is very little reporting that is not environmental. Therefore, environmental reporting includes coverage of health, economics, politics, commerce development, physical resources and a wide variety of scientific research. In short, people's interactions with the living and non-living components of their environment, which after the environment by using, redistributing or disturbing its resources, constitute a topic for environmental reporting.

Isn't it interesting in my opinion a successful environmental journalist besides being all this has to be an activist, who must be prepared to go beyond the confines of his "beat". He has to have interaction with several NGOs; social-action groups, voluntary bodies and grass root movements, besides the Ministry and Departments of Environment in the Union and the state governments.

This interest and surge in environmental reporting the world over is also because environmental factor has begun to play an increasingly important role in world development. As has been pointed out by the UNEP Executive Director, Mostafa Kamal Tolba, in the publication, *Sustainable Development: Constraints and Opportunities* : We have made rapid headway among the decision makers who work in government, the UN agencies and the development assistance agencies. Few, if any, in those cabals would put a contrary case that development which takes no account of the environment is worth pursuing. At the launch of the World Conservation Strategy, the then UK Environment Secretary, Michael Heseltine observed that 'in any individual decision' the starting point will be : conserve what matters – those who have a contrary objective must bear the onus of proof.

In creating this transformation several organisations have made significant contribution. The foremost, of course, is UNEP. The coordinating, catalytic and stimulating role of UNEP the world over is too well known to need any recapitulation here. Suffice to say that its publication, information and awareness programmes have always been most helpful in building up proper perspectives. ECU of the ESCAP has been catalytic in organising Asian Forum of Environmental Journalists as also the national fora in different countries. Its publication, Reporting on the Environment, is a valuable source of guidance, for all those working in this area.

With the body of material built up by different institutions the world over, and precious perspectives gained in creating environmental awareness through media, environmental reporting is slowly making a place for itself.

The number of NGOs, voluntary groups, academic and corporate bodies and social activities, taking interest in environmental issues has increased significantly in recent years. As Rahul Gupta points out : The environment will no longer be the concern of merely professionals, ecologists and rebels who are eternally questing for a cause. A new breed of seekers have joined the ranks of the ecologically conscious college students. The subject is at last being incorporated in the regular curricula.

Because of the wide ranging issues involved and the edge of activism, environmental reporting scenario is becoming more topical and interesting : hot and interesting. The Earth Summit at Rio turned out to be a battle ground between the rich and the poor. It was an all out war between the rich nations of the North and the poor in the South. On the question as to who should pay for the Development, Bahuguna says in Development Redefined :

> The Earth Summit in Rio, which has raised high expectations among the people of a basic change in the prevailing development system may end in a fiasco as it has fuelled a

> North-South, in other words rich poor controversy. The rich countries, which are the main culprits in creating environmental hazards, want to stop certain activities which are responsible for these. The poor, on the other hand ask : Why should we sacrifice our development when we are not the culprits? The rich should pay for the programmes proposed to be launched in the poor countries to control environmental pollution. The rich on account of their wasteful life style have improvished the earth and simultaneously created dust, smoke and noise.

Environmental issues are progressively taking a holistic perspective, including the increasingly consumeristic life styles, development paradigms, as symbolised by big dams are being challenged. Bahuguna has highlighted this aspect as under :

> Protection of environment should not be seen in isolation. Similarly, conservation is not possible till we adopt a life style, which had been developed for generations and reflects the wisdom of the people. Wisdom is the collection of experiences, which common people have gained for generations.
>
> No generations have made new additions to it. This traditional wisdom has been ruthlessly suppressed by the modernity, which is based upon a philosophy of development with economic growth. In the religion of economic growth, market is temple, the technocrats and experts are the priests and dollar the God. This has taken humankind on the brink of disaster. Remote mountain areas are the frontiers, which have till now protected our natural heritage, specially mountains, glaciers, forests, rivers, meadows, etc. Modernity looks into these as a commodity and utilizes these to accelerate the pace of economic growth. This is exacting the pound of flesh.

Another interesting aspect is the involvement of women in environmental concerns. Writing in the introduction to the Women, Ecology and Health, issue of *Development Dialogue* 1992 (1-2), Shiva says :

> It is now twenty years since the 'environment' was put on the agenda of international concern with the Stockholm

Environment Conference in 1972. The United Nations Conference on Environment and Development (UNCED) held in Rio de Janeiro in June 1992 marked the culmination of these two decades of environmentalism, enabling us to take stock of trends, to build on the most promising and lasting ones.

The global concern for planetary survival has moved from issue to issue in the last two decades. From desertification it shifted to acid rain, and the current preoccupation is the pollution of the atmospheric commons, symptomatised by the greenhouse effect and ozone depletion. The official environmental response has largely been one of offering technological and managerial fixes which, rather than addressing or solving the basic ecological problems, often create new ones. The search for technological fixes to the greenhouse crisis is an example of a cure which could be worse than the disease, destabilising the planet's life support systems and livelihoods in the Third World.

There is another response to the growing ecological crisis which comes from women engaged in the struggle for survival; because of their location on the fringes, and their role in producing sustenance, women from Third World societies are often able to offer ecological insights that are deeper and richer than the technocratic recipes of international experts or the responses of men in their own societies. There are two reasons for this.

Firstly, these responses come from cultures in which maintenance of life has been the civilising force; secondly, the gender division of labour, introduced or aggravated by the development process, has increasingly pushed women to work for the production of sustenance, while men have been drawn into military and profit seeking activities.

Environment, as an issue, is already on the international agenda; media must continue to take sustained and informed look at it.

REFERENCES

Aggarwal, Anil (1989). Environment – A bleak landscape. *Gentleman*, February 28, 1989, pp. 90-101.

Adiseshiah, Malcolm S. (1989). Plan to preserve the environment. *Yojana*, Vol. 33 (14

& 15) : 28-33.

Bahuguna, Sunder Lal (1994). *Save Gangotri* in Save Himalayas; Chipko Information Centre, Silyara, Tihri Garhwal, India, p. 20. ibid : Development Redefined p. 38.

Dahlan, M. Alwi (1989). The environmental approach to mass media coverage. *Media Asia*, 16 (4) : 219-222.

Gupta, Rahul (1994). Environment in Syllabus. The Green Book, *Financial Express*, 23 October.

India Today (1986). Deforestation–An environmental holocaust. *India Today*, 15 August, 1986, pp. 73-87.

Shiva, Vandana (1992). Women, Ecology and Health : Rebuilding Connections in *Development Dialogue* (1-2), p. 3.

Tolba, Mostafa Kamal (1987). *Sustainable Development—Constraints and Opportunities.*

9

Distance Education and Media Technologies

USHA CHANDER*

Trained manpower throughout the world, and more so in industrial societies, is becoming a precious resource. With the growing eliticism of the centres of training and education, the universities in most of the countries are in the danger of becoming redundant and insignificant, as they cater to the privileged few. The recent trend towards free market economy, has also made more and more countries realize the need for providing an easy access to affordable higher education to the masses.

In developing economies like India, with its growing population and aspirations, where the resources allocated for education cater to a wide spectrum from providing basic primary education to vocational education, non-formal education, adult education and where higher education forms only one component, the realization has not dawned too soon.

According to Kulandaiswamy (1993), backwardness, economic or social, has unfortunately inherent in it a perpetuating potential. Countries that are underdeveloped and backward have difficulties in liberating themselves from such a state of existence. Nevertheless, their only salvation lies in empowering people with knowledge.

Whereas conventional higher education institutions as they by and large, serve the purpose, there is a need to replace or transform into a new system where everybody, regardless of sex, income, age, social status, geographic location, linguistic barriers can have access

* Secretary, Development Communication, India.

to quality higher education to meet contemporary social needs and demands. Now this can also be an ideal recipe for a vast country like India with its own characteristic circumstances.

The distance education system, which is already nearly three decade old was conceived to meet just this demand. But the question is, has it developed and grown as projected? Will it be able to realizc the ultimate goal of education for all by the turn of the century? What is the role of media in distance education? All these issues need to be deliberated and discussed.

Higher Education and Need for Distance Education

In the agricultural economy, education was an ornament and an embellishment, it was not an economic necessity. It became a tool for development in the industrial economy; and now, knowledge is a resource by itself.

A review of the progress of education would reveal that distance education is the third stage in the evolution of education, the first two stages being the *Gurukul* system of the past and the classroom system of the present. The Academy of Plato and the Lyceum of Aristotle being the Greek versions of the ancient *Gurukul* system of India. Under this system, the students lived with their learned teachers or *gurus* and imbibed knowledge. While it was a very good system and appropriate for those days, it had its own limitations in the scope of the subjects taught, range of facilities and accessibility to sought-after teachers.

The later form of higher education was institution based and was established by the scholars who earlier taught a handful of disciples. While this system could cater to more students, it could not keep pace with the growing demand. Moreover, with population explosion and dwindling resources in the education sector, it was becoming uneconomical too. Therefore, came the need for the classroom system which did not replace the earlier one, but absorbed and incorporated in it additional dimensions. But again it was not enough.

It was under these compulsions that the Open University and the distance education system was born (Kulandaiswamy, 1993). Distance education today has come to be accepted as well recognized as a mode of education relevant to and necessary for meeting the emerging demands of today. The emergence of science and technology as a dominant force, not only in economic development, but in human affairs in general and the dawn of the knowledge era, as many choose to call the present period, have brought education onto the centre stage as never before in human history. The classroom system has become inadequate to meet the challenges. Such terms as universal education, continuing education and equity in educational opportunities, are concepts and demands that form the buzz words today.

The increasing social and economic value of training and education has made it a pre-requisite for each and every type of attainment, irrespective of its levels. The numbers involved are large, the cost implications are high and the composition of the target group is many orders of magnitude different from the thin layer of the social stratum from which the past generation of students came. A new system to meet some or all the new demands was the mandate for distance education, especially in the developing countries where accumulated arrears have to be cleared; gaps developed over centuries have to be reduced if not closed completely.

While distance education as a system itself could be called rather young, only around 25 years old, it is blooming not only in Asia, but also in Western Europe, United States and Canada. As per the studies conducted by the NIMME of Japan in the Asia and Pacific region; and by ICDO of Open University UK in Africa and Latin America for UNESCO, distance education is a much needed system for continuing education in the third world countries. As these countries are striving for development and new technologies are being inducted into their society, the need to catch up with new knowledge and upgrade skills has become essential for survival in the competition.

Strangely, education has still remained a craft, the content in education improved, but the conduct of classroom instruction continued to be the same. The teacher is still writing and laboriously drawing on the blackboard what is already available in the book. There has been no significant increase in productivity. There has always been a linear expansion in input to increase output when needed.

Concept of Continuing Education

Prof. H. Kato, Director General, NIMME in his keynote address delivered at Teen Murti House on 'The Use of Communication

Technologies for Distance Education', in Japan said that continuing education was a key concept in countries like Japan. Establishment of 'Lifelong Education Bureau' in the place of earlier 'School Education Bureau' on the recommendation of the Central Educational Board was a step in the right direction for his country. This Lifelong Education Bureau had a broad framework covering not only continuing education, primary education, secondary education but also kindergarten. The main concept was to look at human life as a continuous process of learning from birth to death.

A country like India will also benefit if it were to follow a similar rationale. Such an apex body could help streamline education system in the country and render education at every level more meaningful in the context of the next level.

In other words, while the conventional higher education institutions will continue to exist, there is a need to replace or transform them into a new system where everybody, regardless of sex, income, age, social status, geographic location, linguistic barriers can have access to quality higher education. Facilities are being added to the new system to give it flexibility and make it more attractive like the credit transfer system leading to easy transfer of a student from one University to another, or even from the open university system to conventional university and vice versa. In other countries, Open University Federations are emerging. In Canada, there is an institution COL, in England there is the International Centre for Distance Learning and in Norway, the International Centre for Distance Education.

In Asia, we can find newer educational opportunities adopting the distance learning system. Higher educational institutions for distance learning like the Allama Iqbal Open University of Pakistan; Japan's University of the Air, Indonesia's Terbuka Open University, Thailand's Sukhothai Thamathir Open University and Indira Gandhi National Open University in India, have been set up. All these institutions of distance learning, apart from their individual characteristics, do indeed have one aim in common; to serve the needs of adults seeking to upgrade their qualifications, career development or to acquire a real understanding of the selected subjects.

Conventional Education System

The conventional education system :

- is locked in space, time and tradition;
- is institution based i.e. the schools, colleges and universities are important;
- is physically and temporarily binding : the buildings, the campuses, the programmes are fixed and the schedule of the classes are time-bound;
- is not standardized : the number and the quality of teachers is limited and may change from time to time;
- is exacting on the student : the student would have to appear for the examination at a stipulated date and time;
- is costly and time consuming;
- is also elitist in nature, in the sense that it is accessible only to upper and middle classes of society;
- is non-participatory : the learning period is decided without any prior consideration of the pace at which a student is able to absorb the inputs; and
- is based on full time study with face-to-face communication in the classroom, mediated through the full time teacher for implementation. Most of the time, the teaching and learning process is centered around the teacher, student, chalk and blackboard.

The conventional system works under several limitations : limitation of subjects that a student can learn, limited number of students admitted, limited number of years to complete the learning process, limited sessions, limited interactions (most of the time, it is one way interaction). In short, it is institution and rule centered education. The learning process of each and every student has to be tailored as per the requirement of the institution. The very purpose of education could be defeated this way.

Correspondence Education

It can be termed as first step to liberate the learner from the clutches of the rigid conventional system and accommodate those who would like to learn more or continue their education. In this system :

- the uses of classrooms, chalks, blackboards, teachers are minimal;
- most of the interactions are through printed or cyclostyled materials; and
- the learners' pace to absorb the subject matter was recognized and the system made flexible enough to help the students grow at their own pace.

Distance Education

This is an improved system on correspondence education. This system is an innovative educational system using all the available and possible means of communication and superior to correspondence education which uses only printed material. It has liberated the learner from the age old printed material in a very special way by supplementing learning materials through other channels of communication and is a part time, home-based study employing multi-media for teaching.

Open Education System

The latest evolution in the system of education is what we call 'open education system'. This system not only incorporates all the flexibilities of correspondence and distance learning systems but liberalizes the education further by relaxing admission requirements, examination and evaluation systems, grading systems, teaching and learning systems, etc. The distance and open learning systems often overlap, thus we may use the terms interchangeably.

Distance education, as such, should not to be seen as one competing with the conventional and correspondence systems of education. Considering the requirement of manpower and the target groups that the two systems can serve, both can coexist and, in fact, complement and supplement each other. The expertise and the infrastructure available in the conventional universities can be utilized for developing multi media packages for the distance education system. And the products thus developed are shared with the students of the conventional universities for greater efficiency and effectiveness.

It is in this context that distance education assumes importance and relevance. This has become possible mainly due to breakthrough in communication technology. The new education policy recognizes the importance of distance education, envisaged it as an alternative form of education to meet the challenges in education for it can synthesize communication technology with the educational demands.

Media Technologies

After great revolutionary changes in industry and transport in the preceding centuries, the twentieth century witnessed dramatic developments in yet another key area : Communication.

Graduating from the printing press, newer and sophisticated media were invented like the radio, television, telephone, computers, cable, satellite based communication, etc. The search was for quicker, more accessible, more user friendly technologies with wider reach. For a while, these new technologies competed with one another and with traditional modes of communication like interpersonal, folk, theatre, etc. But soon, towards the close of the century, one witnesses the trend towards merging of technologies, integration of various media with the choice of interface being left to the audience.

This is significant because it often appears that some where along the line, during all this striving for excellence in technology, the main end user was forgotten.

Paradoxically, while there was a virtual 'Information explosion' during the century, the education and literacy levels were registering a new low everywhere. The population figures, however, shot up leading to a basic question whether the far fetching developments of the nature witnessed in communication technology were really desirable. In a scenario where information was not equally shared by all and became to be symbolized as power and controlled by the mighty and powerful, the very purpose of developing new technologies was defeated.

Overall education standards began to fall and higher education, or education which could lead to better paid employment, became priced commodities. The advantage tilted in favour of the elite, those with purchasing power. The market driven economy had cast its influence on education too.

The present decade has witnessed leapfrogging developments in the history of electronic communication in India. Since 1990s television has received unparalleled attention as a medium of distance education. Due to rapid expansion of communication networks throughout the country, television has now become a legitimate concern of educators and media planners.

Starting with a few transmitters in 1982 (New Delhi, Asian Games), the number of transmitters in the country has now jumped to 562 covering 84 per cent of our population.

School Television made its debut on the Indian educational scene about three decades ago in 1961 as an organized, systematic and sequential support to formal school instruction, with the aim of contributing to improved teaching of science, though its use was later on extended to the teaching of English and Mathematics. The primary school telecast was undertaken in Delhi after 14 years, in 1975. Later on, various educational projects were launched to supplement primary school education. Enrichment programmes are now being telecast through the national network for which the topics are usually selected from the primary school curriculum. School television programmes are telecast for students of two age groups—lower age group, and 9 to 11 years (upper age group). These programmes are viewed through community sets installed by the Central as well as State Governments.

Various countries of the world have adopted school television to solve a variety of educational problems. A study conducted on a sample of 100 schools from nine districts of Rajasthan into the attitude of TV custodian teachers towards STV and the relationship between the teachers attitude on the one hand and their job satisfaction on the other indicated the following :

Most custodian teachers had adequately favourable attitude towards STV; 59 per cent of the respondents were either favourable or highly favourable to STV and 37 per cent were either unfavourable or highly unfavourable to STV.

Teachers appreciated STV as a tool for teaching (teacher concern) and presentation of content (tele-teacher concern). They were, however, less enthusiastic in accepting STV as a tool of learning for students (student concern) and were quite articulate about the limitations of STV (television concern).

Teachers' attitude towards STV was independent of their personal and academic characteristics. However, there was a moderate and statistically significant relationship between teachers' attitude towards STV and the classes taught by them. Teachers who taught classes IV and V showed more positive attitude towards STV.

Unlike traditional technologies, newer ones have special attributes like greater interactivity, a much higher degree of technological sophistication, knowledge–intensivity and greater accessibility in advanced societies. Their emergence has a significant social impact. The obsolescence rate (i.e. the rapidity with which the technology in question gets obsolete and gets replaced) is higher. While the potential and possible applications of these newer technologies are immense, their effective and equitable utilization for the welfare of mankind is a challenge by itself.

Traditional media like writing, printing and electronic media like radio and TV are essentially one way media and their interactive capabilities are limited. Moreover, the limited interactivity is not live or spontaneous but occurs after a considerable time gap.

The emergence of the new forms of electronic media like teleconferencing is of particular interest for distance learning because of their interactive capabilities. The use of electronic media components as an essential part of the multi-media approach to distance learning has always been a dream for those in the field especially in a country like ours.

Teleconferencing is an interactive electronic communication among two or more locations. The punch word here is interactive and it is indeed this quality of interactivity that really distinguishes teleconferencing from the conventional one way media like broadcasting or narrowcasting (V. Rama Rao).

Teleconferencing is an already accepted form of technology in advanced countries, especially for business communications. It is only a matter of time for this technology to become popular in countries like ours, as necessary infrastructure like telephone links and satellite are already available. Usually, the attraction for adopting teleconferencing is said to be the savings it results in minimizing physical travel. The time-saving involved in this process is also a significant factor. Experience of advanced countries in which teleconferencing is in wide usage shows that apart from economy and time saving, this technology improves corporate efficiency and enables participatory management.

Distance Education is a child of the revolution in Communication Technology. The distance education system operates in a distance teaching learning mode. The teacher and the taught are almost never face-to-face. The learner is usually provided with a multi-media course material package. The content and treatment of the curriculum is such that the teacher is built into the text. There are numerous Check Your Progress and Activities alongwith Self Assessment Questions, to enable the student to pause, think and evaluate his own comprehension as he is proceeding to learn.

Various media deployed in distance education are print; audio; AIR (Broadcast)/Cassettes (Narrowcast); video : DD (Broadcast) cassettes (Narrowcast); satellite : audio teleconferencing/video teleconferencing. In addition, tutoring, counselling and practical exercises at the Study Centres nationwide form an integral part of the distance learning approach. The use of multi-media approach in this system makes learning an interesting and enjoyable experience in addition to reducing the time spent on learning.

While a significant portion of the study material is in the print form, the audio video component plays a vital role. In fact, it is this new dimension that differentiates the open learning system from the correspondence system. The reasons for including the electronic media and even computer based technologies in the distance education is rooted in the fact that they are eminently suited to carry higher education to the doorsteps of the masses. In fact, they may be the only hope to provide easy access of higher education to all who yearn for it.

While the audio and video cassettes are primarily produced for the distribution to the students and to the study networks, the government owned mass media channels like the Doordarshan and AIR have earmarked regular time slots for broadcasting such software. The satellite technology available in the country is also being considered for use in distance education. Some preliminary experiments have been conducted by IGNOU in collaboration with ISRO in this direction recently.

Mass Education : Teaching Shops to Teaching Industries

The industrial civilization was ushered in by the end of the 18th century; since then there has been an increasing use of science and technology to improve productivity in every field and craft has been gradually replaced by technology. The mass production technology is now being extensively used for teaching/learning purposes. Some writers characterize it as industrialized form of education. This system has many of the characteristics of the industrial enterprises like rationalization, division of labour, mechanization, assembly line operations, standardization, etc. They form very important features of the distance education system. The system is also more capital intensive, unlike the conventional system which is more labour intensive. It is these factors that influence the nature of its administrative structure and generate contradictions which require careful attention.

The nature of learning materials production and the nature of learners may pull the administrative system in different directions. The capital intensive, industrialised form of operations of distance education gives rise to centralization of operations. The planning and designing of courses is centralized. The production of learning materials is also centralized. This is done to meet the needs of mass production, standardization, specialization and accompanying mechanisation. This process results in top heavy administration and high dependence on modern technology i.e. printing machines, electronic equipment, etc.

The distance learner profile pulls the system in a different direction. The dispersal of the clientele groups is an important feature of distance education system. The study centres – local units of distance education administration – provide a link between these widely dispersed students and the university. These centres play an important role in providing support services to the students. This demands more and more decentralization of the system resulting in inherent contradictions in the demands on the administrative system of distance education. The nature of learning material production process results in the centralization of operations. On the other hand, the nature of learners' demands decentralization of services. Balancing these contradictory pulls poses a challenge to the system.

In the distance education, the knowledge and skills of teacher are transmitted to large mass of learners through the use of technology i.e. print, audio visual, radio and television. The use of technology for mass production of knowledge has a propensity for uniformity. The diversity – differences in age, experience, skills, levels of achievement of distant learners demands diversity in treatment. As a result, there is a contradiction between uniformity of products of technology and diverse needs of the learners.

The Teacher : From 'Humble Guru' to a Hi-tech Manager'

With the emergence of this system of education and in keeping with its own peculiarities and characteristics, the role of the teacher has also undergone radical changes. As there were no students to face, the teacher had to learn to teach by remote control. The teacher had to build a part of himself into the printed text. This was a challenging task but has proved to be possible. The simple classroom aids had to be envisaged in audio/video formats and produced after careful planning. The limited time when the teacher and the taught came into direct/indirect contact (either during a counselling session or in an extended contact programme or through teleconferencing), a lot of prior communication and planning had to be carried out at both ends to make the interaction truly meaningful.

Besides, the teacher had to possess the desirable qualities of a good manager, a good coordinator, a good planner, a good counsellor and a good visualizer to be able to cope up with the new system. Some other attributes like technophilly and confidence in facing the camera are also assets.

The teacher must be able to switch from being a natural teaching to a packager of knowledge into capsuled information. The teacher's role has now widened in scope from being a mere dispenser of knowledge to a knowledgeable guide.

The universities of the future may be tailored to cater to such demands. The courses offered should cover a wide spectrum of areas and offer a flexible package of course structure and content for the learner to learn at his/her own pace (Kato, 1992).

The flexibility of the distance learning system is helpful in designing and developing courses which are socially relevant and technically up-to-date. It helps in maintaining uniformity in various courses. Irrespective of their socio-economic background or geographical location, the students under distance learning system have access to the same learning material.

It enables the learners to get the benefit of new knowledge which is being generated and accumulated at a rapid pace. Dissemination of knowledge through face to face interaction between teacher and learner is time consuming and quite often results in diffusion of outdated and obsolete information. Because of the use of latest communication technology in the distance learning system, latest information and knowledge can be disseminated to the students. It enables the learners to receive information from sources who are most knowledgeable and has the expertise in developing self-instructional learning material.

Thus, the learner is not bound down to one teacher as in the case of conventional system of education. Unlike the conventional system of education where the benefit of education is restricted only to those who are registered students and attend classes, the use of communication technology, particularly the broadcast media, benefit even those who may not be enrolled as students. Various courses offered enable the students to select courses which will be most relevant to their needs. The distance learning system also allows specialization in different professional fields. The University of Pondicherry has started experimenting with such concepts.

Moreover, the drastic reduction in costs has made it possible to tailor curricula for different chosen groups. This would have been virtually impossible and extremely unviable earlier, thus depriving a section of the population from the benefits of education in newer emerging areas.

Education For All : A dream to be realized soon

The industrial civilization was ushered in by the end of the 18th century; since then there has been an increasing use of science and technology to improve productivity in every field and craft has been gradually replaced by technology.

Distance education provides the key as it is technology oriented, has higher productivity, and, therefore, comparatively cost effective, which is a factor of great significance and promise for the developing countries. It has endowed education with almost unlimited flexibility in glaring contrast to the rigidities inherent in the conventional system, and has also removed its 'temporal' and 'spatial' limitations.

As we stand towards the end of the 20th century we find that it is easier to transport knowledge to people rather than transport people to the place of knowledge. This reversal, though apparently simple has as great a potential as human imagination and ingenuity can see in it.

Profile of a Student in the 21st Century

If one analyzes the trends in new communication technology and its resultant impact on distance education, one can almost certainly picturise the student in the next century. This breed will certainly undergo a radical change and will not be comparable with their counterparts today.

It is very tempting to picturise the profile of students in the future. Let's try...

A student may not necessarily conform to a particular age group, sex and social strata. Acquiring any kind of education will be more like any other commercial activity. Admissions may not be a problem for any course and the restrictions, if any, may be more in the nature of affordability. There may not be a campus or a building to go to attend classes. Instead all communications and interactions would be through telephones either directly or via computers, television, cable, satellite or a combination of more than one of these. The student from affluent background may be owning the equipment of communication while a disadvantaged student may be hiring or using a public facility. There will be a choice of teachers, experts, subjects, activities, technology interface and tremendous scope for experimentation and original thinking and independent learning. Another important factor would be that one can learn at one's own pace. One can transcend the spatial, temporal and physical limitations between the teacher and the taught faced at present.

Is everything going to be as easy, simple and rosy? The answer is No, because the most vital link : the human touch, the interpersonal interaction will be missing and will be missed, for all its worth. It will become a priced commodity and reserved for the privileged few.

Prior to the efforts of IGNOU, the UGC through its countrywide classroom project has been using television to impart quality education to the undergraduate college students. The countrywide classroom of UGC started its telecast from August 15, 1984, with one hour educational programmes. Now most of the programmes are produced indigenously by EMRCs and AVRCs. Initially UGC was using more foreign made programmes for its countrywide classroom. The programmes telecast through the country wide classroom are to enhance the learning system of the conventional college students.

Apart from UGC, the Dr. Ambedkar-Open University of Andhra Pradesh uses radio broadcasts to teach the enrolled students.

The improved channel of communication malses the distance learning system more open. The open learning system uses the following communication channels to impart knowledge in addition to the lifting of all unnecessary restrictions.

1. The printed material – written in a special format devised for the students of distance education system.
2. The audio and video programmes – to make the students clarify and reinforce what they have already learnt through the printed material.
3. The broadcasts through radio and television do the same thing as audio and video programmes do. They add more knowledge by fine tuning what the students have already learnt.
4. The computer system is another channel which reinforces the knowledge.
5. The counselling sessions at the study centres bring in the human touch, the face to face communication element in the distance learning educational system.
6. The assignments which give the idea to the students whether or not their learning process is in the correct path. And if yes, how correct they are.

One thing has to be remembered here that all the elements employed in distance education have accumulating effects, though it may seem that these elements are repetitive.

There is no doubt that in India distance learning system is urgently required to educate our people. Like any other third world country, India lacks facilities to develop its human resources. Probably, this is the only system by which the largest possible number of citizens can be accommodated for training and development in the shortest possible time with minimum resources.

REFERENCES

Dighe, Anita. Assessing the effectiveness of the audio/video programmes for diploma in management. Module I-A communication study.

Kulandaiswamy, V.C. (1993). Distance education in the Indian Context. IGNOU, New Delhi.

Malik, P. S. (1987). Distance education in Indian, in *Distance Education in Asia and the Pacific – Vol. II*, Assian Development Bank, Manila, pp. 35-37.

University Grants Commission – Country-wide Classroom–A Window on the World.

10

Asian Perspective, Significant Milestones and Watchdog Mechanism

Whereas themes like Rural Development, Empowerment of Women, Sustainable Environmental Development, National Unity, and media strategies to aid and enhance the effective implementation of these issues and programmes have been on the national agenda for several years now, as also various aspects of information society and its socio-cultural impact in the country, the issues of immediate relevance which have lately engaged the attention of media scholars and policy-makers include : the Asian Identity, Asian perspective of communication issues, Entry of foreign press – whether it should be allowed or not, and the flip-flop attitude of the Indian government; and Regulating transnational and satellite broadcasting. It would also be in order to focus on some of the successful communication models and significant milestones which have been innovative and inspiring in harnessing media technologies for the larger social purpose. This wide spectrum presents us with the variety and complexity of the communication scenario obtaining at present.

The Asian Identity

> Asia, long known as a continent of contrasts, is today increasingly seen as a continent of change – as the continent of the coming century. It is a continent of increasing literacy and life expectancy, of rising expectations and changing life styles, of growing affluence and urbanization, of wider media coverage and greater exposure to the world. The tidal wave of progress which started in East Asia and advanced across

> Southeast Asia is now lapping at the shores of north and south Asia.
>
> A recent report on, Asia in the year 2000, states that the continent which now has half the world's population will have over two-thirds by the turn of the century. All but four of the world's largest cities will be in Asia. The number of affluent Asian households will rise by 50 per cent to over 51 million. And Asian per capita GDP will double.
>
> In step with these changes and contributing to them, are the Asian media. The number of daily newspapers and magazines show, an upward trend. The number of households with TV sets has increased by 70 per cent in the past five years, compared with 6.7 per cent in the U.S. Radio ownership has also registered phenomenal growth. But it is satellite broadcasting, notably Asia Sat I, which has dramatically altered the Asian media landscape, leading to a deregulation of media markets, changing patterns of advertising expenditure and creativity. (Vijay Menon)

Asia has at long last started to define itself. Asian consciousness and identity are coming vigorously to life. Western nations are increasingly impressed by the economic power and the political gravity of the region. But Asia's success in the far-ranging and relative terms of global competition should not obscure those forces, in internal and absolute terms, now authoring a cohesive Asian worldview. Asian corporate culture is starting to exert its equalising effects. Meanwhile, the cultural links between the middle classes of various Asian countries are strengthening through the power of electronic communications technology. .... The Hong King based Star Television Network was quick to create an Asia wide entertainment network. Under pressure from Star TV, Indian public television has fought back by broadcasting Japan's hit drama series, "Oshin," now shown in 30 countries, most of them in Asia (Funabashi, 1994).

The above extracts subsum the emerging identity of Asia-Pacific. Asia is being noticed as never before. The enhanced media status – information technology, satellites, television programmes – has been a subject matter of a large number of papers, seminars and conferences. Writing about the emerging media scenario, Deodhar (1993) says :

A modern era of satellite based personal communication and mobile services is dawning today and voice, video and data services via satellite will contribute to the realisation of the global village concept. Some firmly believe that satellites will become the great homogenisers of mankind.

Space over Asia is becoming prime property. The booming economies of many Asian nations like India, China, Indonesia and Malaysia and their prosperous and demanding middle class has fueled a very high degree of interest in satellite communication services. There is so much demand that there are already confrontations over choice orbital locations in geostationary orbit.

AMIC – Promoting the Asian Perspective

AMIC, the Singapore based media organisation, has been making significant contribution in the areas of communication research, documentation, publications, seminars and institutional development.

In this context, Menon (1987) observes : Today, the world is turning towards Asia; the West wants to visit the region, get to know it better and invest here. As such, the focus of communication is becoming increasingly more complex. Communication is, in the final analysis, the key element that can foster greater cooperation on both the regional as well as international levels. A concerted effort must be made and maintained to foster communication which, in turn, will foster greater harmony.

The story of AMIC is the story of an organisation reaching out not only with information about mass communication in the region but also with teaching, training and research inputs, aiding in a greater appreciation and use of mass communication as a tool to help the countries of Asia face the challenges and avail of the opportunities of the information age.

Menon adds : The Story of AMIC began in 1971. It was set up primarily as a regional documentation centre in response to a suggestion from UNESCO. A graceful building on Newton Road was made available to the centre and AMIC was in business. Mass communication documentation is still an important activity at AMIC. But the range of activities has grown. AMIC has been fortunate in getting both moral and material support from the Government of

Singapore and the Friedrich-Ebert-Stiftung, an independent foundation in the Federal Republic of Germany. UNESCO, which has conferred on AMIC recognition as a Category 'B' NGO, continues to provide valuable encouragement and assistance. Specific projects are funded by various organisations around the world. It is a non-governmental organisation and a non-profit foundation.

AMIC has initiated and coordinated various national and regional applied communications research projects. Of AMIC's role in the role of research, the distinguished scholar, John Lent, had this to say:

> Mass Communication a slow start in Southeast Asia, as it generally had been in the third world....Virtually all aspects of communication had gone unstudied....The boon to the development of mass communication as a field of study, not only in Southeast Asia but all of Asia was the Asian Mass Communication Research and Information Centre founded in Singapore in 1971. . . . The role of research has been featured in nearly all AMIC seminars and conferences.

AMIC's Publications Programme produces Media Asia, a quarterly for media practitioners, Asian Journal of Communication, a bi-annual scholarly journal, and Asian Mass Communication Bulletin, a newsletter containing news and information on current media trends as well as bulletins on AMIC activities. In addition, the publications unit publishes books, monographs and occasional papers.

For the past several years AMIC has introduced some very successful programmes; both at the Asia-Pacific level–Annual Conference which draws a galaxy of communication professionals, administrators and policy makers; as also in-country programmes where participants drawn from diverse disciplines : print journalism, mass communication, extension education, electronic media, sociology, interact in seminars and conferences.

AMIC, in short, has been a fore-runner in Asia in pioneering communication research, training and publication programmes.

Entry of Foreign Press

An issue which has polarised the media community, overheated the debate on the subject, with both the protagonists and the opponents speaking on the move with almost religious fervour. The opinion amongst the members of the Council of Ministers seems to be divided. Those favouring the move consider the step as the logical outcome of the on-going process of liberalisation, whereas those opposing advise caution against going blind folded into an unknown area and cite the 1955 cabinet decision disallowing such entry as sacrosanct.

Cultural imperialism, foreign invasion, patriotism and values under siege, access to more information, these and other cliches are doing the rounds in media circles. Our media are now-a-days facing an issue as important as the spiked defamation bill which was introduced by Rajiv Gandhi. The only difference is that at that time the media were one and now they are dispersed. The imminent entry of the foreign press has raised the hackles of not only the politicians but also some journalists. The issue has been raised in the Parliament, taken before the judiciary and has been the subject of passionate and heated debate in the columns of the press.

The raging debate over the issue has divided the media as well as the politicians into warring camps. One group feels that the foreigners are coming here only for ravaging our five thousand year old culture and traditions. They are the evil incarnate who are all set to subvert our social and secular fabric. Now, their eyes are set to stop us from our onward march ahead. Gaining entry into India is an excuse for the cultural imperialism of the country. Profit may not be the only criterion for the press coming to India. There can very well be propaganda and power. Many European countries do not allow the foreign press to operate from their soil, so why should we?

The second point is that no one is powerful enough to destroy our deep-rooted and ancient tradition. Are we so weak or our culture so fragile that it can be plundered so easily? Moreover, if the foreign media come they will bring better and newer technology resulting in superior publications for the consumers to choose from. The foreign media have no axe to grind and are here only for the purpose of expanding their business. They will create more job opportunities for Indian journalists. The foreign media cannot operate on their ground rules but have to function within the periphery of the rules laid down by the government. Thus, these are incapable of subverting our national interest.

The reality is that both sides are motivated by mercantile gains. Protagonists of the move say that the opponents use the facade of patriotism and culture to save their media interests, since they are dishing out mediocrity and shoddiness, they feel threatened of competition. Moreover, foreign newspapers and magazines are allowed in the country without any import duties which shows that we are not unknown to the views of the foreign press. In fact, India has a chance of becoming the media and the information centre of the entire South Asian region. The foreign press can do a lot to improve our depleted image abroad. Recent trends show that the information industry is fast on its way to becoming the largest industry in the world. Foreign press is going to bring in competition and newer technology which will go a long way in providing a choice to the consumers.

The opponents of this move say that already foreign television has cast a detrimental effect on the younger generation who are being swayed by a culture alien to us. Moreover, we do not need competition as we have more than enough of internal competition. The entry of foreign media is going to affect the small and the vernacular press and not the English language press. Our ethos and culture are such that we live in the environs of compassion and not cut throat competition. Such a condition is not congenial for our interests and culture.

This debate involves two warring camps of different cultural ideologies, thinking and perspectives. People involved are perched on different sides of the cultural fence. Any decision by the government affects the interests of both the groups. If the foreign press comes then some of the media barons tend to lose so they use the camouflage of culture under threat. If it does not come, in that case someone else's economic interests are affected so they hide behind the attractive face of market economy.

Regulating Satellite and Cable Television

The phenomenal growth of satellite and cable television in India during the last three years has been a subject of serious debate and concern, thereby leading to the constitution of expert committees to make an indepth study of the issue and introduction of the Cable

Television Networks (Regulations) Bill, 1993 so as to regulate the operation of cable television networks in the country.

The satellite and cable TV virtually stormed the Indian homes, more so the upper middle classes in the metropolitan towns and big cities, ever since the coverage of the Gulf War in 1991 by CNN. Since then there has been no looking back – infact it is a steep uphill progression all through – increasing number of cable operators, households with cable connections, programmes and channels. This dramatic expansion in satellite and cable television networks gave rise to almost simultaneously, loud protests and serious concern on account of adverse socio-cultural impact of western programmes and the persistent neglect of studies by students. The Government of India constituted a committee of eminent media experts headed by a senior officer from the Ministry of Information and Broadcasting, K. A. Varadan. The committee observed : While the relevance of these programmes to our views as they are at present telecast may be questioned, this development has some disturbing implications. No country can afford to sit back passively and let some foreign agency decide what kind of programmes should be broadcast to the people of the country. At the same time, it is neither desirable nor feasible to stop these transmissions or ban their reception.

The committee also recommended arrangements to be made under which the programmes put out by the licensees are continuously monitored to ensure that prescribed guidelines are not violated. It suggested that a single statutory/autonomous body known as the Broadcasting Council of India envisaged under the Prasar Bharati Bill be assigned the task of laying down guidelines and monitoring the quality of programmes, send out warnings and suggest punitive action in cases of violation of the guidelines, etc. The Government of India subsequently introduced a legislation in the Parliament in August 1993. The Bill provides for a registering authority, takes recourse to the programme code and the advertisement code, to be framed under the Act. It has also been made mandatory for the cable operator to transmit at least one Doordarshan channel of his choice through the cable service. However, it has been felt that the thrust of the proposed legislation is towards making it a tool for regulation rather than providing an approach to develop cable television as a social and economic resource.

In this context, the guidelines formulated by the Working Group

I at the AMIC/BES Seminar on Legal and Regulatory Aspects of Satellite Broadcasting held in India in October 1993 provide useful inputs for formulating policy and legal framework governing transnational broadcasting in the region. The Working Group observed :

> Despite the negative effects of satellite broadcasting, regulation is not the answer. People should have the right to choose what programmes they want and when. Regulating programming content would only increase demand for it as in the "forbidden fruit". Therefore, it is desirable to provide the people with as much freedom of choice as possible in the media. The content of transnational broadcasting can be made more acceptable by an international convention incorporating universal values. SAARC and other regional associations should take initiative in this direction.
>
> The emphasis of the effects of satellite broadcasting as a "cultural invasion" need not cause concern in the SAARC countries as we have a rich cultural heritage. Some amount of tolerance may be necessary for society to "absorb" the potentially negative effects of foreign programming.
>
> SAARC countries should take initiative to cooperate against the universally accepted negative effects on culture of satellite broadcasting. There is a need to develop an appropriate code of ethics that will promote responsibility and ethical standards in transnational broadcasting.
>
> National programming in the respective countries should be improved in terms of quality. Competition should be encouraged. Privatisation should also be considered on option. Particularly, news programmes should establish more credibility with the public by providing timely and accurate reporting of events.

The implications of Cable Television Networks (Regulations Bill) were discussed at a seminar organized by NAMEDIA Foundation under the aegies of FES in August 1993. Most of the participants in the seminar suggested wide ranging changes in certain provisions of the Bill before these could be implemented. The need to encourage talent and produce good quality programmes to meet the challenges of cultural invasion from foreign satellite networks was stressed. The eminent journalist, Chanchal Sarkar stated that the menace of cultural alienation, induced by the western programmes, could be curbed only through making good programmes. He hoped that in due course of time media professionals in the country would be able to achieve high professional standards and wean away the audience from foreign programmes.

An interesting offshoot of the sudden and large scale entry of foreign satellite networks has been that it has made Doordarshan sit up.

In India the victim of instant communication has been Doordarshan. Satellite transmission not only made communication easy and instant but also brought in competition. In the aftermath of the Ayodhya incidents, DD realised that it was futile to suppress information or delay it. It is ironical that on December 6, 1992 news which were relevant to the Indians were being relayed to them by BBC and CNN while DD was fiddling. Those days are a part of history when the government controlled media could delay information without people being aware of it.

Now-a-days DD is making strenuous efforts to improve image, not because it wanted to but because it is being forced to, because it is not only losing it's viewers but advertising revenue as well. The earnings from sponsors and advertisers are rapidly increasing for foreign TV networks. Satellite TV has an advantage over DD in the sense that it has been successful in attracting upper section audiences with soaps like *Santa Barbara* and *The Bold and the Beautiful*. Its advertising rates are lower than those of DD. Alcohol, cigarette and jewellery ads are banned on DD which bring in a lot of money for foreign networks. Zee TV, a purely entertainment oriented channel, is weaning away DD audiences because it is a song and a film based channel. Recently it was in the race with DD for telecasting the budget speech for which DD ultimately had to tie up with this channel. It was an important occasion as this budget was being keenly debated and discussed and none of the networks could afford to miss.

An interesting outcome of this multiplicity of channels is that the advertisers and the media planners are in a dilemma. The approximately 15 TV channels confuse them no end, which channel or particular programme would bring the best returns. They realise that audiences have been lost in numerous channels. Earlier the media planners had one broadcasting agency -DD and they had an inkling what would click with the audiences. So they only would decide on the timing of the ad as well as its duration. The message would be driven home and the vehicles were serials like *Ramayan* and *Buniyad*. Now things have undergone a change as target audiences have scattered. The prospective buyer could be hooked to any one of the multiple channels. One of the viable options left for the media planners is to go by the television ratings of the programmes if they have to reach out to the desired target audience.

All these changes which took place within a span of a couple of years have vastly modified the Indian media habits. Viewers, readers, media planners, advertisers and any one who is directly or indirectly concerned with the media have undergone a change in media behaviou.

Significant Milestones : Successful Communication Models

SEWA : Empowerment of Women, Demystifying Video

The SEWA, led by the well known social activist, Ela R. Bhatt, has pioneered several innovative programmes in the areas of empowerment of women, dymystifying video technology for articulating grievances of women construction workers, vegetable sellers and other self-employed women, and helping them in poverty alleviation programmes. SEWA provides a forum to the deprived and disadvantaged section of women for collective social action.

The SEWA has gone a long way in innovating several such self-help programmes like opening bank accounts for the illiterate women account holders and providing credit and marketing facilities, apart from initiating them into social action. These women workers also learnt to operate and handle video camera and record their protest programmes. When one such programme – how to organise for collective social action – duly video taped was shown to their counterparts in Lucknow, the latter became so enthused – looking at the natural gestures and expressions of demonstrating women, that they also straight away decided to embark upon a similar programme at Lucknow. Such was the efficacy of innovative and imaginatively conceived social programmes using video technology as the major input.

The success and accomplishments of the SEWA, alongwith programme like *Grameen Bank* of Bangladesh and Sarvodaya of Sri

Lanka, has inspired the deliberations of South Asia Poverty Alleviation Programme of SAARC which had been made as one of the regional issues at the Colombo Summit in 1991. Besides waging struggles for higher wages, improved working conditions and social security benefits, SEWA has also been working on developmental activities. As chairperson of the National Commission on Self-Employed Women and Women in the Informal Sector appointed in January 1987, Ela Bhatt, in the report "Shramshakti", made an indepth study in relation to the Communication Network Systems. Some of the relevant recommendations regarding women programmes and radio, video and communication support systems are :

> It is recommended that taking cue from the grass root organizations, video be used as a consciousness raising tool by telecasting programmes which give information and guidelines in a visual manner. Further appreciating the power of songs sung in traditional tunes, but having feminist content which is very effective in mobilizing women, Doordarshan should collect such songs in collaboration with activist groups and prepare video cassettes to be played in the programmes of *Ghar Bahar* and *Krishi Darshan*.

The findings of the Commission during its tours indicated that the radio is more popular with women and comparatively, they have more access to it. It is recommended that careful planning in the use of information dissemination be done. Further, it is very necessary to reschedule the timings of the programme. Only those women who are not working can listen to the radio in the afternoon. Most of the women workers prefer to have relevant programmes in the late evening.

Use of communication media in aid of a process of raising community participation or for that matter, participation by self-employed women, in development programmes, could be viewed in terms wider than mere information dissemination exercises. Most development programmes which visualize the self-employed women as the potential beneficiary or one of the intended target groups would need to accord a broader orientation to communication support systems. Communication support systems for the development programmes must reach the intended beneficiaries in terms of their own communication matrix and in a manner which provides a comprehensive effect, access to information, skills in using the information and ability to articulate feedback which may ultimately make the policy formulation processes much more meaningful.

Kheda Communication Project (KCP)

The KCP, which has been extensively documented, received the prestigious UNESCO Prize for rural communication in 1984. The project is an ideal illustration of local, decentralized television broadcasting, effective in ushering in social change in rural area. The ingredient of success : audience participation, identification of specific issues of interest and relevance to the village community; political autonomy from Central Government and support from state government. The KCP symbolises the lessons learnt from SITE and is an effective illustration of what a decentralised and participative communication programme can do as a catalyst for social change and rural development.

Detailing some of the important aspects of this unique experiment, Contractor *et al*. (1993) point out : Organizationally, the Kheda Project was a decentralized unit. It relied heavily on government funds for financial support, thus making it independent of commercial interests. The Kheda Project enjoyed a great deal of political autonomy from the central government. The organization fostered a participatory form of management, recognizing the fact that individuals working at various levels in the organization were often the most qualified to suggest improvements. The Kheda Project encouraged a high level of lateral communication between production, research and administrative staff. Organizational members were encouraged to attend training workshops in their respective skills (many of which were organized by SAC).

The success of the KCP lies in its close collaboration with extension agencies involved with dairying, agriculture, health; dymystifying approach of those working at the Project, and social content of the programme. In a way the Project came to represent the poorest section of the rural population which looked upto it as their Project. Referring to the philosophy guiding the programme, Kumar says : The focus of the Kheda Communication Project has, however, not been so much on the diffusion of technical innovations, but rather on : exposing the oppression and bondages in the present social and economic system in such a way as to heighten understanding, mobilising the community and the individual himself to break away from these bondages and promoting self-reliance among the individuals and the community.

Development, therefore, to the Kheda team, implies a break from the *status quo*, from inertia; it implies movement, change. And change requires a certain attitude, motivation and, of course, appropriate physical and social infrastructure. It implies, moreover, social change, education, awareness, and of course, economic development – which cannot take place in isolation.

They believe that communication can play a major role in accelerating development and their attempt in Kheda is to use TV – and also to supplement it by other means – for development in the broadest meaning of the term.

India could certainly do with more such projects, which would harbinger the message of change and development in the remote rural areas of the country.

Rural Telephony and Kittur Village

The question whether telephone is more important or drinking water earlier, frequently voiced in the meetings of rural development planners is becoming increasingly redundant. The village population, conviced of the efficacy and necessity of telecommunication facility, as an aid to economic and social activity has started clamouring for more telephones. The evaluation of the impact of introduction of telephone in the Kittur village in Karnataka state as given in the Information Revolution in India, brings out interesting revelations.

Kittur is a village in Karnataka state in South India with a population of 12,500. This village served as a pilot project in which a 128 line RAX, developed by C-DOT, was installed in mid 1986. The 74 subscribers comprised local farmers and small businessmen. They averaged an amazing 2400 calls per telephone per year. An evaluation of the impact of the 74 telephones in Kittur found an 80 per cent increase in cash deposits at local banks, an increase of 20 to 30 per cent in local business incomes, and easier, more rapid access to medical doctors for local residents experiencing health emergencies. The evaluation survey found that Kittur villagers reported several benefits of rural telephone service which included :

savings in time and money, higher prices for agricultural products, increased sales of farm products, quicker medical attention, increased social interaction with friends and relatives and faster information and news flows.

Telephony in Kittur was so popular that neighbouring villages demanded a similar telephone service. The Kittur experience with the automatic rural telephone exchange was hailed as a success.

The Kittur project and C-DOT's other researches, have facilitated the perception of Indian telephones as being something of a business necessity rather than a luxury.

The above three illustrations of use of video technology, television and telephone for social change and awareness, national development and economic uplift do bring home the view point that modern communication technologies can be used for socially relevant and purposive programmes. It is their application, however, for entertainment and commercial exploitation purposes primarily which has given rise to wide spread and legitimate concern.

Media Watchdogs

The media structure in the country severely need watchdog mechanism and media monitors so as to make media subserve the larger social purpose rather than that of the government of the day, which more often than not, use the media apparatus, particularly the electronic media for partisans ends and party propaganda. The urgent necessity of public accountability of the media through national bodies constituted of professionals, public persons, activist groups and voluntary organisations has been felt for a long time.

1. National Council for Mass Communication

One of the earliest proposals of the Chanda Committee to the implementation of which the government had actually agreed was the formation of the National Council for Mass Communication. As envisaged, such a Council would be a well-informed representative and broad based body comprising officials as well as eminent non-officials to advise on the role and performance on the mass communication media, including their coordinated growth. The Chanda Committee also visualised the Council to be autonomous body and not subordinate to the Ministry of Information and

Broadcasting. It should have the professional status to advise the Government on policy for all media of communication, traditional and modern, and on future developments such as satellites, cable TV and others. Representatives of the press, publishing, advertising, films, and of the union and state governments must find a place on the Council.

Masani (1976), enlarging on the concept of the National Council for Mass Communication, suggested that the Council should also ensure coordination between the media and the agencies responsible for development policies including the Planning Commission, the Ministries and departments of Government. It could usefully undertake manpower planning for the media and provide for the evaluation of their performance particularly the programmes of social education. Masani's observations succinctly sum up the situation of broadcasting in the country as under :

Broadcasting cannot play any significant role in our lives unless there is clear thinking on a mumber of issues. Indian public opinion has to be mobilised to play a much active part in deciding what kind of broadcasting it wants and what its role should be, particularly in supporting the great national tasks. The present confusion of aims and contradictory policies, undisputed and unchallenged by the public, save in the most perfunctory manner, are retarding the growth of broadcasting.

The National Council will go a long way in meeting the above objectives and also in educating public opinion about the imperative need of inculcating a healthy broadcasting culture in the society.

2. National Council for Listeners & Viewers – An Audience Watchdog Boody

It is being increasingly realised that only a strong public opinion, articulated through properly constituted forum representing a broad cross section of society, like Media Advocacy Groups, Public Interest Organisations or other media watchdog mechanism could play an interventionist role in ensuring healthy and creative media programmes.

The Korean television audiences have constituted 'Task-force groups' for concentrating on specific areas of broadcasting such as children programming, entertainment, news and advertising, group members are concerned about broadcasting law, objectivity and fairness of news coverage, violence in children's programmes and commercialization of sex, gender discrimination, etc. TV monitoring is being undertaken by such groups through training courses for the staff and volunteers of other interested organizations.

In Britain there is a Viewers' and Listeners' Association and Radio and TV Committee in which writers and academics are represented. Such groups like Media Advocacy Groups can certainly play useful role in sensitising public opinion against objectionable and pernicious trends in TV programming. Whenever, public opinion through an organised representative forum asserts itself the government has to take note of their perceptions.

In this context, Rao (1988) has pointed out : A monopoly should entail restraint by the monopolists as well as responsiveness to public demands and needs. Both Doordarshan and viewers must interact. It is time that people in general and viewing households in particular came together to "talk back" to TV as moderators of the system. When rail passengers and telephone subscribers can form groups to protect their collective interest all over India, why not a TV Viewers' Council of each TV Centre? It is odd that despite its ubiquitousness, TV has not generated a consumer movement of its own. As a result, the public dissatisfaction with TV can only increase. Autonomy or no autonomy, the need to "talk back" to TV is immense. Keeping television relevant, responsive, democratic and progressive is a matter requiring the constant vigilance of all viewers. Television should be kept from feeling it is infallible and invulnerable and so from becoming tyrannical. Public scepticism towards it is a vital ingredient in improving its quality.

3. Broadcasting Council

Of late, there has been renewed emphasis on establishing Broadcasting Council which was earlier envisaged by the Prasar Bharati Act 1990. The Act under section 15, stipulated that the Broadcasting Council would receive and consider complaints from :

> 15 (i) any person or group of persons alleging that a certain programme or broadcast or the functioning of the Corporation in specific cases or in general is not in accordance with the objectives for which the Corporation is established;

> 15(ii) any person (other than an officer or employee of the Corporation) claiming himself to have been treated unjustly or unfairly in any manner (including unwarranted invasion of privacy, misrepresentation, distortion or lack of objectivity) in connection with any programme broadcast by the Corporation.

The Varadan Committee, set up by the government for the regulation of satellite and cable TV, suggested that this body (Broadcasting Council of India) be entrusted with the functions in respect of licensing of cable network operators, as against the option of the government issuing licences for a new channel, as well as monitoring and quality of programmes.

Stressing the imperative need and urgency of establishing a watchdog mechanism, Sevanti Ninan (1994) said : Clearly some kind of watchdog body is needed to end the practice of allowing every Minister of Information and Broadcasting who comes along to treat Doordarshan as his personal *jagirdari*. The Puri telecast was supposed to be interspersed with a direct telecast of the *Rath Yatra* in Dhenkanal as well, a town that needs no introduction since Singh Deo put it firmly on the national map. And the whole thing was preceded by a curtain raiser after the news on Thursday which pushed off the air the scheduled programme for that hour. And that was not all either. When Singh Deo was in the U.S. addressing some kind of NRI Oriya association in New Jersey that merited a special programme too. It is not just the minister, it is also his party. Narasimha Rao's third year in office required major *chamchagiri* on DD's part and we suffered through it. Is State-owned TV supposed to serve the ruling party and its minions or the people? Silly of me to ask, I should know the answer, but may I suggest we viewers attempt to change the answer to that question?

Of late there has been little talk of setting up the Broadcasting Council, a watchdog body that was to have been constituted as part of the legislation on Prasar Bharati. But increasingly as vulgarity on television increases, as misuse of airtime increases, as public grievances against TV channels both indigenous and foreign proliferate, public and legislative pressure needs to be built up to set up such a council so that we can have the accountability that it can bring out.

Instances of misuse of electronic media, violation of the

guidelines governing the News Policy for Broadcasting Media, have been documented and commented upon on numerous occasions, with hardly any redressal.

4. Mass Media Social Audit

Inspired by the experience of his association with the Social Audit Panel of the Ministry of Communication, the eminent media expert, N. Bhaskar Rao (1994) has suggested setting up a similar panel for the mass media with the help of teachers across the country. Rao says : I find school principals and teachers around the country are alarmed at how they are losing control over children but the government is a helpless spectator to the bombardment from the sky of satellite TV programmes. Newspapers everywhere are going in for television and you are going to see media conglomerates. There is, therefore, great need for professional monitoring and analysis of the media scene, keeping the social aspect in mind. Troubled by the recent phenomenon of the use of telephone by the youngesters for sex and astrology services for getting "telefriends", Rao hopes that volunteers in different parts of the country who are not connected with advertising would come forward to work on the panel. Explaining the concept further, Rao says : New technology has come in many areas but the rules have not changed to keep pace with it. The same thing is happening in mass media. Technology is overtaking us. We shall have to develop a methodology of social audit of mass media to monitor the role, impact and the way it is used.

It is essential to ensure that media technology does not subvert the moral and ethical values; and adversely influence the minds of impressionistic younger generations.

5. Franchise Stations

Not a part of media watchdog mechanism, the enormous potential of utilizing franchise stations for education, teaching and training purposes has been repeatedly stressed at various fora. As Dua (1980) points out : So far very little is known in this country about the purpose and functions of such franchise stations. In western countries, especially the United States, the departments of journalism and mass communication of nearly all universities operate at least one radio station, a television centre and a film studio. These media are exclusively run and operated by students of journalism and mass communication departments. Reporting, writing and broadcasting and also conducting the affairs of radio and television stations are part of academic instruction and training for mass communication students.

The Working Group on Autonomy for Akashvani and Doordarshan, while recommending the institution of franchise stations stated :

> We accordingly recommend that the National Broadcast Trust be authorised to grant a broadcast franchise, whether for radio or television, to approved educational institutions. Such a franchise recommendation by the National Broadcast Trust should automatically be converted into a broadcast licence by the Ministry of Communications, the specific frequencies being allocated and coordinated by the Ministry's Wireless Adviser.
>
> We see several advantages in developing a system of franchise stations on the lines indicated. These would not only bring variety and innovation to programming but would give a powerful stimulus to educational and extension broadcasting. They would enhance participation and access and involve young people in broadcasting as well as in the development of hardware and software systems and of communication policy. These broadcast stations could be used as internal teaching aids as, for example, by the departments of medicine and engineering, education, communication and journalism, and by the physics and electronics faculties. The cultural faculties of universities would also be able to use the broadcast facility to enhance the creative talents of the student community.

The franchise stations for agricultural universities would go a long way in reinforcing the extension work of the universities, apart from teaching and training purposes which could also be fulfilled through such stations. Kheda Communication Project, run by the Space Application Centre, has successfully shown as to how such communication development programmes can be successfully executed. The National Workshop on Akash Bharati convened by IARI (1978), while endorsing the recommendations of the Working Group said :

The Workshop accepted the recommendations of the Working

Group on establishing Franchise Stations in institutions like Agricultural Universities, Central Research Institutes and other institutions which have an educational, extension or cultural orientation.

There should be a continuous inflow of information on achievements of proven value in terms of research and extension communication covering problems for the benefit of the various rural people for increasing the farm production and also helping in better living. Regarding the question of the franchise stations being permitted to relay news bulletins or commercial advertisements, the workshop recommended that the developmental news may be broadcast, in the form of Farm and Home Round-up twice a week or so.

In summary, it would be worthwhile to consider implementing the above recommendations and instituting franchise stations for training and academic purposes.

REFERENCES

Bhatt, Ela R. (1988). Shramshakti. New Delhi : National Commission on Self-Employed Women and Women in the Informal Sector.

Contractor, Noshir S., Arvind Singhal and Everett M. Rogers. (1993). Satellite Television and Development in India : A Utopian, Dystopian, Neutral and Contingency View. *Perspectives on Development Communication.* New Delhi : Sage.

Deodhar, P. S. (1993). Space over Asia is fast becoming prime property. *Sunday Observer*, 20 March.

Dua, M. R. (1980). Themes in Indian Communication. New Delhi : Metropolitan.

Funabashi, Yoichi (1994). At last, the Asianisation of Asia. *The Asian Age*, 25 February.

Gupta, Rahul (1994). Entry of Foreign Press—Media Highly polarised. Participation in Seminar on Entry of Foreign Media, New Delhi; 23 February.

Khanna, Harish (1993). Seminar on the Legal and Regulatory Aspects of Satellite Broadcasting. New Delhi : AMIC Seminar Report, 21-23 October.

Masani, Mehra (1976). Broadcasting and The People. New Delhi : National Book Trust.

Menon, Vijay (1993). Editorial. *Media Asia*, 20(3) : 122.

____. (1987). Regional Cooperation and Mass Communication Information in Asia : Role of AMIC. Handbook of Libraries, Archives and Information Centres in India.

Ninan, Sevanti. (1994). Misuse of airtime. Media Pulse. *The Hindu*, 17 July.

Rao, Bhaskara N. (1988). Public role in improving TV. *Times of India*, 6 September.

Rao, Bhaskara N. (1994). *Times of India*.

Singhal, Arvind and Rogers, Everett M. (1989). *India's Information Revolution.* New Delhi : Sage.

Varadan Committee (1992). Summary of the Report. *Communicator, XXVII* (1) : 14-17.

Epilogue

After this work was completed, and while the manuscript was being readied for publication, several developments have taken place that, in a way, bear association with the analysis and trends reflected in the book.

Two distinct trends are gathering speed. A sustained campaign against foreign media entry and drive to combat vulgarity in media. The ordinance on Cable television, inauguration of the first information super high way, abandoning of Doordarshan's channel 3 have also been subjects of animated discussion during the last two months.

In a rare show of solidarity, the Press Council of India, major media and civil liberty organisations, intellectuals and eminent journalists have made a concerted effort to thwart the entry of foreign print media in the country. There is near unanimity that the cabinet resolution of 1955-56, imposing a ban on the entry of foreign media should not be lifted or erased. It has been emphasised that print media should not be made a play thing of crass commercialisation, saying that, "newspaper is not a product, but an interplay of news, views, ideas and other elements."

In an impassioned article : Foreign media inside the Indian fourth estate*, V.R. Krishna Iyer, says : To commoditise the media and allow their foreign manufacture within the country is fraught with grave risk to our sovereign democracy and nationalist survival. After all, freedom of the press is but a derivative from the fundamental freedom of expression under Article 19. Freedom of

* *Times of India*, 29 October 1994.

speech and of occupation or business belong only to Indian citizens and are subject to reasonable restrictions "in the interests of sovereignty and integrity of India. . . . friendly relations with foreign states, public order, decency or morality or in relation to contempt of court, defamation or incitement to an offence." No 'open sesame' for an outside news heavy weight can be mindlessly granted. He further adds : There is nothing in national life which cannot be shaken or shaped by alien agencies once they get a foothold. To caricature or debunk Indian events and developments and make the world outside hostile to us is an easy process once the foreign barons are in. Moreover, a tremendous expansion of information and communication with its manipulable effects, makes the culture and conscience of our people a victim of the foreign (Indian) media. Their commercial conquest of our economy and their influence on people's tastes and interests and values are so complete that the excesses in which they indulge for control of the minds and markets makes one tremble.

In any case, majority of the considered opinion is veering round to the view that since the press is an integral part of the modern constitutional state, the fourth estate; foreign participation in a news medium is a virtual infringement of national sovereignty.

Several organisations, groups and academic institutes are involved in undertaking studies and mobilising public opinion regarding violence and vulgarity in the media. These include the National Human Rights Commission, National Commission for Women, Centre for Media Studies, Indian Institute of Mass Communication, NGOs, academics, social workers and women activists. The objective is to sensitise public opinion against the rising trend in crime, violence and vulgarity as a result of film based programmes and cultural alienation through television programmes. Now that we are entering the phase of 'gavel-to-gavel', television programming, as in the O J Simpson case in the United States; 61 channels and round-the-clock televiewing, it is all the more important that an informed and assuring public opinion is brought to bear on the efforts of Ministry of Information and Broadcasting to check objectionable trends in electronic media. The new ordinance for regulating cable networks, promulgated in September this year is the first step towards professionalising cable TV systems. The ordinance as pointed out by Amit Agarwal* has been able to achieve

* Cable Networks : On a Slow Burn, *India Today*, 31 October 1994.

several objectives. The cable operations are now legal and have three years period at their disposal to upgrade their systems to specifications. The ordinance also makes it mandatory for cable operators to adhere to the prescribed programme and advertisement code. Whereas it is yet to be seen as to how effective implementation of the ordinance would be, particularly with reference to applicability of codes and inspection by officers of the Central Government; the ordinance is as Agarwal rightly points, "like a speed-breaker at the entrance to an information superhighway."

The raging controversy over the cabinet decision to review Channel-3 has brought forth strong media reaction : A choked channel, Death of Channel III, Second thoughts on DD-3 are some of the newspaper headlines. The crux of debate is : the government is too scared to allow a forum for "free and frank discussion, representing all shades of opinion from the saffron to the red." Mourning the death of Channel III, the eminent media critic, Amita Malik says : Alas for Doordarshan and the future of TV in India. This is a body blow from which perhaps it will never recover. Since our lot seems to be precensored, sanitised and canned news and comments. And you know what that means. Death of Channel III.*

The Third Wave, as Alvin Toffler had titled his earlier book, or as his latest book, Powershift : Third Wave money increasingly consists of electronic pulses. . . . Third Wave money is information, the basis of knowledge; is gathering accelerated speed in the country.

Nandu Pardhan points out in New Frontiers, New Horizons : During the recent outbreak of plague in the country, doctors in India effectively used the Internet to communicate with their foreign counterparts. A heartening development indeed, realised by networking technology.

India continues to operate at two levels : struggling with the problem of rural literacy, rural transport, health and hygiene; as also high-tech world of networking, interactive video conferencing and information super highways. And both the trends would continue to gather strength in years to come.

---

* *Indian Express*, 24 October 1994.

Bibliography

Acharya, R.N. (1987). *Television in India*, New Delhi : Manas Publiacations, p.44.

Agee, Warren K. (1969). *Mass Media in a Free Society*, New Delhi. Oxford and IBH Publishing Co.

Akash Bharati : National Broadcast Trust vol. 1. (1978) – Report of the Working Group on Autonomy for Akashvani and Doordarshan, New Delhi : Ministry of Information and Broadcasting, p. 108.

AMIC (1985). *Satellite Technology : The Communication Equaliser*, Singapore.

An Indian Personality for TV Vol. 1. (1985). Report of the Working Group on Software for Doordarshan, New Delhi : Publications Division, pp. 116-121.

Anjana Maitra, Sinha (1993). *Women in a Changing Society*, New Delhi : Ashish Publishing House.

Arbind, K. Sinha (1987). *Mass Media and Rural Development : A Study of Village Communication in Bihar*, New Delhi.

Bahuguna, Sunder Lal (1994). Save Gangotri in *Save Himalayas*; Chipko Information Centre, Silyara, Tihri Garhwal, India, p. 20. Ibid : Development Redefined, p.38.

Bhatt, Ela R. (1988). *Shramshakti*, New Delhi : National Commission on Self-Employed Women and Women in the Informal Sector.

Bongartz, Heinz (1993). *Development Theories : NGOs and Self Help Organizations*. Nepal Foundation for Advanced Studies, Kathmandu, p.6.

Chawla, N.L. (1982). Communication Policy in India – Software Production and Distribution. *Communicator*, XVII (1) : 2-6, 10.

Chitnis, E.V. and K.S. Karnik (1983). Technological options help us get what we seek. *Communicator*, XVII (3-4) : 24-28.

Contractor, Noshir S., Arivind Singhal and Everett M. Rogers (1993) Satellite Television and Development in India : A Utopian, Dystopian, Neutral and Contingency View. *Perspectives on Development Communication*, New Delhi : Sage.

Dighe, Anita. *Assessing the effectiveness of the audio video programmes for diploma in management*. Modula I-A Communication Study.

Dua, M.R. (1980). *Themes in Indian Communication*. New Delhi : Metropolitan.

Eapen, K.E. (ed.) (1989). *Role of Radio in Growth and Development*. Bangalore : Mass Media Education, Research and Information Centre.

Etienne, Gilbert (1985). *Rural development in Asia. Meetings with peasants*. New Delhi : Sage.

FAO (1987 a). *The Paradigm of communicaton in development*. From knowledge transfer to community participation – Lessons from the Grameen Bank, Bangladesh Development Communication – A Case Study, Rome.

FAO (1987 b). *Development Support Communication*, Expert Consultation, Rome.

Friedrich Ebert Stiftung, Bonn (1984). *New communication technologies and their impact on western industrialized countries*. Communication manual.

Funabashi, Yoichi (1994). At last, the Asianisation of Asia. *The Asian Age*, 25 February.

Gerbner, George (1988). *Violence and Terror in the Mass Media*. Reports and papers on Mass Communication, UNESCO.

Goonasekera, Anura (1993). Media technology and social imperatives : An examination of communication policies in selected Asian countries. *Media Asia*, 20 (4) : 194-204.

Guback, Thomas and Varis, Topio (1982). *Transnational Communication and Cultural Industries*. UNESCO.

Gupta, V.S. (1981). Communication Planning – A plea for appropriate communication. *Media Asia*, 8 (3) : 156-161.

– – (1983). Indian TV : Software Policy Needed. *Vidura*, 20 (5) : 262-265.

– – (1987). Rural press development in India – Status, factors affecting its growth and future prospects. *Media Asia*, 14 (2) : 67-72.

– – (1989 a). *Rural Press : Problems and Prospects*, New Delhi Press Institute of India.

Gupta, V.S. (1989 b). Case Study of Indian Rural Television : The Krishi Darshan Programme. *Media Asia*, 16 (4) : 215-218.

Guy, de Fontagalland (ed.) (1976). *AMIC Study Seminar on Development Communication*, March 1985 – A Report, AMIC, Singapore.

Hudson, Heather (1989). Information Technology : Challenges for Development. *Development Communication Report*, 4 (67) : 1-2.

India Today 1986. Deforestation – An environmental holocuast. *India Today*, August, 1986, pp. 73-87.

Jain, G.P. (1979). Rural Press. *Seminar* No. 235 : 23-25, New Delhi.

IJayaweera,, Neville d. (1982). Communication Satellites-A Third World Perspective new communication Technologies and their Impact on Western Industrialized counties.s Summary Report of a collquium held in Bonn, 17-19 December.

Jayaweera, Neville D. (1982). Communication Satellites – A Third World Perspective New Communication Technologies and their Impact on Western Industrialized Countries. Summary Report of a Colloquium held in Bonn, 17-19 December.

Josef, Eschenbach (1977). *The role of broadcasting in rural communiation* – Mass Media Manual. Friedrich Ebert Stiftung – Bonn.

Katz, Elihu (1968). Diffusion : Interpersonal influence. *International Encyclopaedia of Social Sciences*, pp. 178-184. The Macmillan company and The Free Press.

Khan, A.W. (1979). Better information through radio for small farmers. New Delhi, *Communicator*, 14 (3) : 47-49.

Khan, Rahat Nabi (1987). The third industiral revolution : An economic overview. *Impact of Science on Society*, 146 : 115-122, UNESCO.

Kulandaiswamy, V.C. (1993). *Distance education in the Indian context*. IGNOU, New Delhi.

Kuppuswamy, B. (1976). *Communication and Social Development in India*. New Delhi : Sterling Publishers Pvt. Ltd.

Lee, John A.R. (1976). *Towards Realistic Communication Policies* : Recent trends and ideas compiled and analysed. UNESCO.

Lerner, Daniel (1968). Modernisation : Social Aspects. *International Encyclopaedia of Social Sciences*, pp. 386-396. The Macmillan Company and The Press.

Luthra, H.R. (1986). *Indian Broadcasting*, New Delhi. Publications Division, Ministry of Information and Broadcasting, Govt. of India.

Masani, Mehra (1976). *Broadcasting and the people.* New Delhi : National Book Trust.

Melkote, Srinivas R. (1991): *Communication for Development in the Third World– Theory and Practice*, New Delhi : Sage.

Menon, Narayana (1976). *The Communication Revolution*, New Delhi : National Book Trust, p. 86.

Menon, Vijay (1987). Regional Cooperation and Mass Communication Information in Asia. Role of AMIC. *Handbook of Libraries, Archives and Information Centres in India.*

Menon, Vijay (1993). Editorial. *Media Asia*, 20 (3) : 122.

Michael Kunczik (1991). *Communication and Social Change.* Friedrich-Ebert-Stiftung, Bonn.

Ministry of Information and Broadcasting (1993-94). *Annual Report.* New Delhi Publications Division, Govt. of India.

Mitra, Anand (1993). *Television and Popular Culture in India*, New Delhi : Sage.

Mody, Bella (1984). Technology Option for Third World countries : Do we have the freedom to choose. *Media Asia*, 11 (2) : 85-89.

Mody, Bella (1991). *Designing messages for development communication*, New Delhi : Sage.

Mowlana, Hamid and Laurie, Wilson J. (1988). *Communication Technology and Development.* Reports and Papers on Mass Communication No. 101, UNESCO.

Nair, K.S. and S.A. White (1993). *Perspective on development communication.* New Delhi, Sage.

Nair, L.R. (1967). Private Press in National Development : The Indian Example in Lerner, Daniel and Wilbur Schramm (eds.) *Communication and Change in the Developing Countries.* Honolulu : East West Centre Press.

Nandini Prasad (1994). *A Vision Unveiled, Women on Television*, New Delhi : Har Anand Publication.

National Perspective Plans for Women (1988-200), New Delhi.

Rao, B.S.S.(1992). *Television for rural development.* New Delhi : Concept Publishing Company, New Delhi.

Rogers, Everett M. (1976). Communication and Development. The Passing of the Dominant Paradigm in : Rogers Everett M. (ed.), *Communication and Development, Critical Perspectives*, Newbury Park, C.A. : Sage.

. . . Sayani Ameen (1993). National and Transnational Censorship – Guidelines and Advertising Codes for Radio and Television. Paper presented at AMIC Seminar on the Legal and Regulatory Aspects of Satellite Boadcasting, New Delhi, 22-23 October.

Sayer, John (1987). Information technology contributes to social change in Asia, *Media Development*, XXXIV (4) : 7-9.

Seminar Report on Doordarshan's Role in Women's Equality and Development.

Shiva, Vandana (1992). Women, Ecology and Health : Rebuilding Connections in *Development Dialogue* (1-2), p.3.

Singhal, Arvind and Rogers, Everett M. (1989). *India's Information Revolution*. Sage : New Delhi.

Srivastava, U.K. (1987). National cost of television in India in the year 2000 – Socio-economic and political implications and issues. *Media Asia*, 14 (3) : 136-148.

Swaminathan, M.S. (1973). *Our Agricultural Future*, Sardar Patel Memorial Lectures. New Delhi All India Radio.

Thomas, P.N. (1993). Information and change in India – Cultural politics in a post-modern era. *Asian Journal of Communication*, 3 (1) : 64-83.

Tiwari, I.P. (1987). *Communication, Technology and Development*, New Delhi : Publications Division.

Toffler, Alvin (1975). *Future Shock*. London : Pan Books.

Toffler, Alvin (1991). *The Third Wave*. London : William Collins.

Tolba, Mustafa Kamal (1987). *Sustainable Development : Constraints and Opportunities*.

UNESCO (1982). *Many Voices, One World*. The International Commission on the Stduy of Communication Problems.

University Grants Commission – *Country-wide Class room-A Window on the World*.

Wang, Georgette (1991). Information society in their mind : A survey of college students in seven nations. *Assian Journal of Communication*, 1(2) : 1-18

– – (1993). Satellite television and the future of broadcast television in the Asia Pacific. *Media Asia*, 20 (1) : 140-151.

Women Still at Receiving End (1994). *The Times of India*, 4 June.

Yadava, J.S. (1994). Communication and Development – The Indian Experience, in Dua, M.R. and Gupta, V.S. (eds.), *Media and Development*, New Delhi : Har Anand Publications.

INDEX

International Communication, 73
IPDC, 103